# THE little pine COOKBOOK

moby

THE little pine

COOKBOOK

modern
PLANT-BASED
comfort

AVERY
an imprint of Penguin Random House
New York

**AVERY**

an imprint of Penguin Random House LLC
penguinrandomhouse.com

Most Avery books are available at special quantity
discounts for bulk purchase for sales promotions,
premiums, fund-raising, and educational needs.
Special books or book excerpts also can be created to
fit specific needs. For details, write SpecialMarkets@
penguinrandomhouse.com.

Library of Congress Cataloging-in-Publication Data

Names: Moby, author.
Title: The Little Pine cookbook: modern plant-based
    comfort / Moby.
Description: New York: Avery, an imprint of Penguin
    Random House, 2021. | Includes index.
Identifiers: LCCN 2020020078 (print) |
    LCCN 2020020079 (ebook) |
    ISBN 9780593087367 (hardcover) |
    ISBN 9780593087374 (ebook)
Subjects: LCSH: Vegan cooking. | Little Pine (Restaurant)
Classification: LCC TX837.M658 2021 (print) |
    LCC TX837 (ebook) | DDC 641.5/6362—dc23
LC record available at https://lccn.loc.gov/2020020078
LC ebook record available at https://lccn.loc.gov/
    2020020079

Printed in China
10 9 8 7 6 5 4 3 2 1

Book design by Ashley Tucker

To the activists who work tirelessly
to make the world a kinder and
more compassionate place.

You inspire me constantly,
and this book is dedicated to you.

MOBY

hearty mains and
large plates 161

desserts 197

drinks 227

# hi, from moby

I became a vegan in 1987, when veganism was so odd and obscure that no one even knew how to pronounce "vegan." (Among the ten vegans in the world, the debate raged: Was it "vee-jun"? "veh-jun"? "vee-gun"?)

In 1987, veganism was synonymous with an almost monastic level of renunciation. We gave up the food we loved in order to live the ethics we embraced.

But as time passed, veganism evolved. By the late '90s, there were high-end vegan restaurants in San Francisco (Millennium), New York (Blossom, Candle 79), and London (Manna), and an almost daily launch of new vegan products. Then, as the twenty-first century unfolded, vegan cuisine started flourishing, eventually proving to open-minded carnivores that it had evolved past its bean-sprouts-and-mashed-yeast origins.

Today, in 2021, veganism is arguably the fastest-growing food movement on the planet. (*The Economist* even pronounced 2019 "The Year of the Vegan.")

Some people embrace veganism as a result of their love for animals. Some people embrace veganism for their concerns about climate change and the environment. Some people embrace veganism for better health. And some people, like me, embrace veganism for all these reasons, but also because the food has become wonderful.

In the early 2000s, I opened my first restaurant, Teany, a little vegan café on Rivington Street in New York's Lower East Side. After I ended my involvement with Teany in 2006, I vowed to never, ever open another restaurant. But then in 2010, I moved to LA and kept noticing a weird building in my neighborhood (Silver Lake) that seemed to be perpetually for sale. It spoke to me.

So, I made an offer on the building, spent six excruciating months turning it into a restaurant, named it Little Pine, and opened it to the public in November 2015.

I opened Little Pine for a few reasons: I wanted a place in my neighborhood where my friends and I could eat; I wanted to create a beautifully designed space, with a beautiful menu and wine list, to show that veganism had "grown up"; and I wanted to generate revenue for animal rights organizations. (I never took a penny from Little Pine, and gave 100 percent of its proceeds to animal rights causes.)

Forgive these (un)humble brags, but we won some awards ("Best Vegan Restaurant of the Year, 2016," *VegNews*), and hosted some of our heroes. ("Oh, look, there's Ellen DeGeneres having dinner with Cory Booker," "Don't make a big deal out of it, but Leo DiCaprio's having brunch with his parents," "Morrissey's here again," "Miley Cyrus is eating with Salman Rushdie?!?") But we always focused on what mattered most: promoting animal rights by serving delicious food in a beautiful space, and reminding people that veganism didn't have to be monastic or punitive…

To that end, some of the recipes in the cookbook are relatively simple, and some are quite involved. But please don't be daunted, as even mistakes can be delicious…

Lastly, I want to thank you. Thank you for your kindness, your activism, and your support, especially during those first few months, when Little Pine was, to put it politely, finding its footing.… I sincerely hope you have a wonderful time with this book, and hopefully I'll see you soon! Thank you!

*moby*

# welcome to little pine

After I moved to LA in 2010, I was driving through Silver Lake looking at the odd and fantastically disparate architecture—the midcentury gems next to auto body repair shops, the fairy-tale castles next to vacant lots, etc.—when I saw what to me looked like a blue art deco battleship. I stopped, got out of my car, took some pictures, and wondered what was going on with this strange, moderne ("e" intentional, as it turns out "moderne" is an odd little post-deco architectural style) battleship/building. Time passed, and I noticed that this weird little battleship building had sprouted a "For Sale" sign. A little niggling voice in the back of my head said, "That sure would make a cute vegan restaurant."

I quickly remonstrated with aforementioned voice, as I'd sworn off restaurant ownership after opening/running/closing Teany in New York. But months passed, and the voice kept quietly saying to me, "That sure would make a cute vegan restaurant."

So on a whim, and to quiet the voice in my head, I called the number for the real estate agent listed on the sign and found out a few things: the building was, in fact, for sale; it was egregiously overpriced; it wasn't currently a restaurant, but it sort of looked like one; no one actually knew the history of the building; and Tim Armstrong of the band Rancid was thinking of buying it and using at as a recording studio.

Some more time passed, and I casually made an offer to buy the building. My offer was casually rejected, and I took this as a sign that I was not meant to own the weird little art deco moderne battleship.

Then, a few months later, I got an email saying, roughly, "The seller has reconsidered, and would perhaps like to sell you their building."

It's worth noting at this point in the story that part of my personal and professional ethos has been "Throw yourself into something and then figure out what you're doing." So I bought the building, having no idea what would actually be involved in turning it into a restaurant. But I knew I loved the building, loved the location, and loved throwing myself into projects that were completely beyond my skill and experience.

The bureaucratic aspects of renovating a restaurant are tedious (turns out that LA has a byzantine and voracious bureaucracy...), but the design aspects were really fun.

In designing Little Pine, I tried to adhere to a few principles: ideally, Little Pine wouldn't look like a traditional vegan restaurant; the design should be bright and vaguely alpine, modern but not synthetic, and not so precious that it would fall apart after a few months; and all the materials used should, of course, be vegan.

So we set to work executing this vision. Months passed, and after the joy of design and the pain of bureaucracy, we had a restaurant!

Oh, one last little detail: All the photographs in the restaurant, even the snowy mountain photos, were taken right here in Los Angeles County.

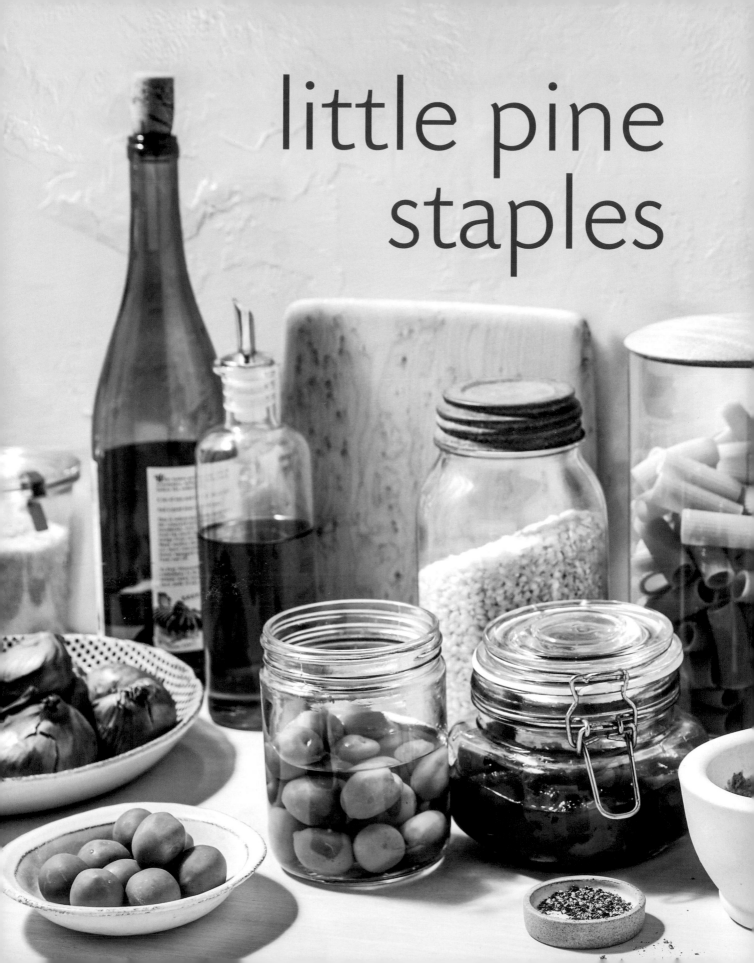

# little pine staples

# hard butter

This vegan butter is perfect for all your baking needs, but it's not recommended for use on toast. (In other words, I wouldn't eat it raw.) You can make it in large batches and freeze it for later use.

**TIME:** 10 MINUTES (PLUS CHILLING OVERNIGHT)

**MAKES:** 4 CUPS

2½ cups refined coconut oil, melted

½ cup unsweetened soy milk

¼ cup sunflower oil

3 tablespoons soy lecithin powder

1  In a high-speed blender, combine the coconut oil, soy milk, sunflower oil, and soy lecithin powder and blend on high speed until thoroughly combined. Pour into an airtight container and refrigerate overnight to harden before use.

2  Store in the refrigerator for 2 weeks or in the freezer for 1 month.

# maple butter

We serve this at brunch, and you should, too. It begs to be slathered on anything and everything you want to smother in melty, gooey butter—especially our croissants (page 64), French toast (page 77), or a steaming stack of flapjacks (page 81).

**TIME:** 10 MINUTES (PLUS CHILLING OVERNIGHT)

**MAKES:** 2 CUPS

1 cup Hard Butter (see above), melted

1 cup pure maple syrup

½ teaspoon kosher salt

¾ teaspoon pure vanilla extract

In a high-speed blender, combine the melted butter, maple syrup, salt, and vanilla and blend on high speed until emulsified. Pour into an airtight container and refrigerate overnight to solidify before use. The maple butter will keep in the refrigerator for 2 weeks or in the freezer for 1 month.

strawberry jam, page 30

maple butter

# cultured butter

To get the tanginess and bite of butter, our chef uses cultured cashew yogurt as the base for this recipe. Drench a bowl of pasta in it, or just be basic and spread it on bread. Simply, it's a great staple that can be used any which way you'd like.

**AHEAD:** SOAK CASHEWS OVERNIGHT

**TIME:** 1 HOUR 30 MINUTES (PLUS SOAKING OVERNIGHT)

**MAKES:** 2½ CUPS

½ cup raw cashews, soaked overnight, drained, and rinsed

⅔ cup water

1¼ cups refined coconut oil

½ cup plain unsweetened cashew yogurt

⅓ cup canola oil or other neutral oil

1 teaspoon liquid sunflower lecithin

½ teaspoon kosher salt

1  In a high-speed blender, combine the cashews and water and blend on high speed, stopping to scrape down the sides from time to time, until the mixture is smooth and creamy and no lumps remain.

2  In a small saucepan, melt the coconut oil over medium-low heat. Add the coconut oil to the blender with the cashews, then add the canola oil, sunflower lecithin, and salt and blend on high speed for about 1 minute, or until thoroughly combined.

3  Line a 6 × 4-inch airtight container with parchment paper. Transfer the mixture to the container and freeze for at least 1 hour, or until firm. Once firm, store the butter in the refrigerator for up to 1 week or in the freezer for up to 2 months.

# garlic butter

I'm not sure this needs much of an introduction, as few things are more obviously delicious than the combination of garlic and butter. We suggest you keep it on hand to use in a variety of dishes, and you can also get creative with it in savory baking or spread it, use it as a dip, fry with it, etc.

3 ounces peeled garlic cloves (about 22)

1 tablespoon olive oil

1 cup (2 sticks) vegan butter

1 teaspoon freshly ground black pepper

½ teaspoon kosher salt

**1**  Preheat the oven to 350°F.

**2**  In a small bowl, toss the garlic cloves in the olive oil to coat. Place the garlic on a baking sheet and roast for about 12 minutes, until soft.

**3**  Meanwhile, in a small saucepan, melt the butter over low heat. Remove from the heat and set aside.

**4**  Transfer the roasted garlic and melted butter to a high-speed blender and add the pepper and salt. Blend on high speed until completely smooth.

**5**  Store in an airtight container in the refrigerator for up to 1 week.

# egg wash

This mixture gives any pastry a decadent shine. (P.S. It contains not a single egg.)

**TIME:** 5 MINUTES
**MAKES:** 1 CUP

¼ cup Bob's Red Mill Egg Replacer

¾ cup water

In a small bowl, whisk together the egg replacer and water until no lumps remain. Store in an airtight container in the refrigerator for up to 1 week.

# cashew cream cheese

If you can eat a bagel without cream cheese, I commend you. To me, this spread makes a bagel a bagel, and without it, a bagel is more or less just donut-shaped bread. Plus, cream cheese is key to all sorts of recipes, both savory and sweet, so if you're operating a plant-based home kitchen, I recommend keeping a batch in the fridge at all times.

**AHEAD:** SOAK CASHEWS OVERNIGHT

**TIME:** 10 MINUTES (PLUS SOAKING OVERNIGHT)

**MAKES:** ABOUT 2½ CUPS

2 cups raw cashews, soaked overnight, then drained

¼ cup water

2 tablespoons fresh lemon juice

1 tablespoon coconut cream

1 teaspoon kosher salt

1½ teaspoons lactic acid

In a high-speed blender, combine the cashews, water, lemon juice, coconut cream, salt, and lactic acid and blend on high speed until completely smooth. You will need to use a spatula to help the mixture along as it blends. Store in an airtight container in the fridge for up to 1 week.

# cashew cream

This is a Little Pine necessity, according to our chef, who says it tastes better than anything you can buy in a store (and I agree). It features in numerous recipes throughout this book, but you can also use it on your cereal or in your tea or coffee—anywhere you'd normally use milk or cream, really.

**AHEAD:** SOAK CASHEWS OVERNIGHT

**TIME:** 15 MINUTES (PLUS SOAKING OVERNIGHT)

**MAKES:** 3½ CUPS

1 cup raw cashews, soaked overnight, then drained

3 cups water

In a high-speed blender, combine the cashews and water. Blend for 2 to 3 minutes, stopping to scrape down the sides as needed, until completely smooth. Store in an airtight container in the refrigerator for up to 5 days.

# cashew mozzarella

When I share meals with friends at Little Pine, they inevitably marvel at our mozzarella, noting that it tastes exactly like its dairy equivalent. It's deceptively easy to make, too. Toss it into a salad, add it to your favorite sandwich, or enjoy it as part of a cheese board spread.

**AHEAD:** SOAK CASHEWS OVERNIGHT

**TIME:** 1 HOUR (PLUS SOAKING OVERNIGHT)

**MAKES:** 12 BALLS

1 cup raw cashews, soaked overnight, then drained

1 cup water

6 tablespoons tapioca starch

¼ cup fresh lemon juice

2 teaspoons nutritional yeast

2 teaspoons kosher salt

1  In a high-speed blender, combine the cashews, water, tapioca starch, lemon juice, nutritional yeast, and salt. Blend for about 5 minutes, until smooth. Pour the mixture into a small saucepan and warm over medium heat, stirring continuously, until the mixture forms a small, stretchy ball. Remove from the heat.

2  Fill a large bowl with water and ice. Using a ¾-ounce scoop, portion the mixture and drop it into the ice bath. Once chilled, wrap each portion tightly in plastic wrap to form a smooth ball. Store in the refrigerator for up to 1 week.

# almond ricotta and smoked almond ricotta

Vegan cheese has come a long way since I became a vegan, as evidenced by this housemade ricotta. It's almost shockingly simple to whip up and, because it's derived from almonds, comes with exactly none of the guilt associated with its dairy dupe. The smoky variety adds unexpected (in a very good way) depth to any dish, and can be especially complementary to greens.

## almond ricotta

**AHEAD:** SOAK ALMONDS OVERNIGHT

**TIME:** 20 MINUTES (PLUS SOAKING OVERNIGHT)

**MAKES:** 2 CUPS

2 cups blanched almonds, soaked overnight, then rinsed and drained

1¼ cups water

1½ teaspoons lactic acid

1½ teaspoons kosher salt

Drain the water from the almonds. Place the almonds, water, lactic acid and salt in a high-speed blender. Process on high, occasionally stopping to scrape down the sides, and blend until smooth. Place the mixture in a nut bag. Squeeze tightly until most of the moisture is removed. Discard the liquid. Store in an airtight container in the refrigerator for up to 1 week.

# smoked almond ricotta

**AHEAD:** SOAK ALMONDS OVERNIGHT

**TIME:** 20 MINUTES (PLUS SOAKING OVERNIGHT)

**MAKES:** 2 CUPS

2 cups blanched almonds, soaked overnight, then rinsed and drained

1 cup water

2 tablespoons fresh lemon juice

1 teaspoon kosher salt

1   Drain the water from the almonds. Place the almonds, water, lemon juice, and salt in a high-speed blender. Process on high, occasionally stopping to scrape down the sides, until smooth. Place the mixture in a nut bag. Squeeze tightly until most of the moisture is removed.

2   Fill the chamber of a handheld food smoker with hickory chips. Place the tube from the smoker in the bowl and cover the bowl with plastic wrap. Turn the smoker on, light the chips, and fill the bowl with smoke. Turn the smoker off and let the ricotta stand until the smoke dissipates. Stir the ricotta and taste. Adjust the seasoning or smoke again as needed. Store in an airtight container in the refrigerator for up to 1 week.

# chickpea meringue

This is the pièce de résistance that makes our Chocolate Pecan Cheesecake (page 211) special, but you can also sub it into any dessert that calls for meringue. It's packed with protein.

**TIME:** 15 MINUTES
**MAKES:** ABOUT 3 CUPS

¾ cup aquafaba (leftover liquid from cooked chickpeas)

¾ cup sugar

⅛ teaspoon xanthan gum

½ teaspoon pure vanilla extract

In the bowl of a stand mixer fitted with the whisk attachment, combine the aquafaba, sugar, xanthan gum, and vanilla and whip on medium-high speed until light and fluffy. Use immediately or transfer to an airtight container and refrigerate for later use; it will keep for up to 5 days. Rewhip the meringue before using.

# coconut whipped cream

Our neighborhood-famous vegan coconut whipped cream is good on anything sweet, including hot chocolate. (Or you can just eat it by the spoonful when you're sad.)

**TIME:** 15 MINUTES
**MAKES:** 2 CUPS

1 cup UHT (ultra-high temperature) coconut cream, chilled

¼ cup sugar

¼ teaspoon pure vanilla extract

In the bowl of a stand mixer fitted with the whisk attachment, combine the coconut cream, sugar, and vanilla and whip on medium-high speed until light and fluffy. Use immediately or transfer to an airtight container and refrigerate for later use; it will keep for up to 5 days.

# gluten-free graham cracker crust mix

We use this as the base for our Banana Cream Pie (page 215) and our Chocolate Pecan Cheesecake (page 211), but you can add it as the vegan foundation to any pie when a crunchy crust is called for.

**TIME:** 3 HOURS 30 MINUTES (INCLUDES CHILLING)

**MAKES:** 5 CUPS

1½ cups gluten-free all-purpose flour

½ cup plus 2 tablespoons packed light brown sugar

1 teaspoon kosher salt

¾ teaspoon baking soda

¼ cup Hard Butter (page 14), cubed and chilled, plus ¼ cup plus 2 tablespoons Hard Butter, melted

¼ cup agave nectar

3 tablespoons unsweetened soy milk

¼ teaspoon pure vanilla extract

Nonstick cooking spray

2 tablespoons granulated sugar

**1** In the bowl of a stand mixer fitted with the paddle attachment, combine the flour, brown sugar, salt, and baking soda and mix on low speed. With the mixer running on low, slowly add the chilled butter and mix until the butter is broken up and the mixture is mealy. Add the agave, soy milk, and vanilla and mix until all the ingredients are incorporated. Shape the dough into a disc, wrap tightly in plastic wrap, and refrigerate for at least 2 hours and for up to 14 days.

**2** Preheat the oven to 325°F.

**3** Lightly spray two pieces of parchment paper with cooking spray. Unwrap the dough and roll it out between the parchment paper into an even layer, about ⅛ inch thick. Remove the top sheet of parchment and transport the rolled-out dough on the bottom sheet to a 9 × 13-inch baking sheet. Bake for about 20 minutes, until the graham cracker is dark brown and firm. Remove from the oven and let cool completely.

**4** Transfer the cooled graham cracker to a food processor and pulse into crumbs. Pour the graham cracker crumbs into a medium bowl. Add the granulated sugar and melted butter and stir until fully incorporated. Use as directed in the recipe of your choice, or transfer to an airtight container and refrigerate until ready to use, up to 2 weeks in the refrigerator or 1 month in the freezer. Bring to room temperature before using.

# caramel sauce
# and fudge sauce

These decadent sauces can be drizzled—or slathered—onto anything you like, including (especially!) ice cream. We use the caramel as a topper for our beloved Banana Cream Pie (page 215) and the fudge sauce in our Chocolate Pecan Cheesecake (page 211) and Chocolate Bread Pudding (page 220).

## caramel sauce

**TIME:** 1 HOUR

**MAKES:** 1 CUP

1½ cups coconut cream

1½ cups lightly packed light brown sugar

1 teaspoon pure vanilla extract

¼ teaspoon kosher salt

In a medium pot, whisk together the coconut cream, brown sugar, vanilla, and salt and heat over medium heat until the sugar and salt have dissolved. Reduce the heat to medium-low and simmer for 15 to 20 minutes, until bubbling and thick. Let cool completely before using. Store in an airtight container in the refrigerator for up to 2 weeks.

## fudge sauce

**TIME:** 20 MINUTES

**MAKES:** 2 CUPS

½ cup coconut cream

½ cup sugar

½ cup unsweetened cocoa powder

½ teaspoon pure vanilla extract

¼ teaspoon kosher salt

¼ cup Hard Butter (page 14)

In a medium pot, combine the coconut cream and sugar and heat over medium heat, stirring, until the sugar has dissolved. Add the cocoa powder, vanilla, and salt and stir until combined. While stirring slowly, incorporate the butter, 1 tablespoon at a time, until completely melted. Remove from the heat. Serve right away or store in an airtight container in the refrigerator for up to 2 weeks.

# flavored syrups

Who needs a $10 bespoke latte when you can make your own fancy syrups at home to add to your coffee drinks? These can also be used as a part of your cocktail—or, in my case, mocktail—bar, as they stir well into any lowball concoction, too.

## ginger syrup

**TIME:** 45 MINUTES

**MAKES:** 1 CUP

⅓ cup chopped fresh ginger

½ cup sugar

½ cup water

In a 1-quart saucepan, combine the ginger, sugar, and water and bring to a simmer over medium-low heat, stirring until the sugar has dissolved, then gently simmer for 30 minutes. Strain through a fine-mesh strainer into a bowl, then let cool to room temperature. Store in an airtight container for up to 2 weeks.

## vanilla syrup

**TIME:** 45 MINUTES

**MAKES:** 2 CUPS

1 cup water

1 cup sugar

½ vanilla bean, split lengthwise and seeds scraped out

In a small pot, combine the water and sugar and heat over medium heat, stirring until the sugar has dissolved. Add the vanilla seeds and scraped pod and simmer for 15 minutes. Remove from the heat and let cool completely. Remove the vanilla pod. Store the syrup in an airtight container in the refrigerator for up to 2 weeks.

# strawberry syrup

**TIME:** 15 MINUTES

**MAKES:** 4 CUPS

1 cup sugar

1 cup water

2 cups strawberries, hulled and halved

**1** In a medium saucepan, combine the sugar, water, and strawberries and bring to a boil over medium heat. Reduce the heat to low and simmer for 10 to 15 minutes, until the strawberries have softened and the liquid is a deep red color. Let cool completely, then transfer to a high-speed blender. Blend until smooth.

**2** Strain the mixture through a fine-mesh sieve into an airtight container, then refrigerate until needed, up to 2 weeks.

# strawberry jam

Few things in life offer such simple pleasure as homemade strawberry jam, which allows you not only to sweeten up your morning pastry but also to reap the health benefits of seasonal berries year-round.

**TIME:** 2 HOURS (INCLUDES COOLING)

**MAKES:** ABOUT 5 CUPS

1 cup sugar

2½ tablespoons apple pectin or citrus pectin

2 pounds fresh strawberries, hulled

1 cup water

1 vanilla bean, split lengthwise and seeds scraped out

1 tablespoon fresh lemon juice

¼ teaspoon kosher salt

¼ teaspoon pure vanilla extract

1  In a small bowl, whisk together the sugar and pectin. Set aside. In a medium pot, combine the strawberries, water, and vanilla seeds and pod and cook over medium heat, stirring occasionally, until the strawberries are very soft and broken down and the mixture is bubbling. Whisk in the pectin mixture and cook, stirring occasionally, until thick and jammy; this can take up to 30 minutes. To check if the jam is ready, take a chilled spoon and pick up a little jam. Hold it above the saucepan and tip the spoon so the jam runs off. If the jam runs off as a sheet, it has reached the set point. If it runs off in drips, it needs to be cooked longer.

2  Remove from the heat. Carefully remove the vanilla pod and discard.

3  Whisk in the lemon juice, salt, and vanilla extract and let the jam cool completely, stirring occasionally to prevent a skin from forming. Store in an airtight container in the refrigerator for up to 1 month.

# hemp seed granola

Sure, granola is a bit on the nose for a vegan, but this one is special. I've had probably thousands of different granolas (granolii?) over the years, and none has come close to our genius pastry chef's genius take on this traditional hippie dish.

**TIME:** 2 HOURS

**MAKES:** 6 CUPS

2½ cups rolled oats

¾ cup almonds, chopped

¾ cup pecans, chopped

¾ cup hulled hemp seeds

½ cup lightly packed light brown sugar

1½ teaspoons kosher salt

½ teaspoon ground ginger

½ teaspoon ground cinnamon

⅓ cup unsweetened applesauce

⅓ cup agave nectar

3 tablespoons pure maple syrup

4½ teaspoons sunflower oil

Zest of 1 orange

**1** Preheat the oven to 300°F. Line a baking sheet with parchment paper.

**2** In a large bowl, combine the oats, almonds, pecans, hemp seeds, brown sugar, salt, ginger, and cinnamon. In a medium bowl, whisk together the applesauce, agave, maple syrup, and oil. Add the wet ingredients to the dry ingredients and stir to combine.

**3** Spread the granola evenly over the prepared baking sheet and bake, stirring every 12 to 15 minutes, for about 1 hour, until the granola is golden brown and looks dry. Fold in the orange zest and let cool completely before serving. Store in an airtight container in a cool, dry space in the pantry for up to 1 month.

# everything spice

Everything spice is a classic crowd-pleasing seasoning that's most commonly used as a bagel topper but can be sprinkled onto just about any savory baked good or dish your heart desires.

**TIME:** 10 MINUTES

**MAKES:** ABOUT 1 CUP

2 tablespoons granulated garlic

2 tablespoons dried parsley

2 tablespoons white sesame seeds

2 tablespoons black sesame seeds

2 tablespoons poppy seeds

1½ teaspoons red pepper flakes

1½ teaspoons onion powder

1½ teaspoons ground turmeric

1 tablespoon freshly ground black pepper

1 tablespoon paprika

In a small bowl, whisk together the garlic, parsley, sesame seeds, poppy seeds, red pepper flakes, onion powder, turmeric, black pepper, and paprika until thoroughly combined. Transfer to an airtight container and store in a cool, dark place indefinitely.

bagels, page 51

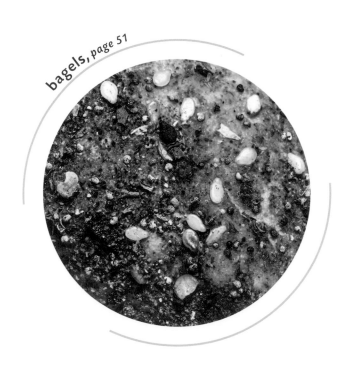

# broth powder

We couldn't find a single broth powder on the market that was good enough for our Potato Leek Soup (page 112), so we made our own. Think of this as a flavor enhancer to be used in soup, stew, or any dish to which you want to add depth. You can also dissolve it in hot water to drink when you don't feel well (we do this all winter at Little Pine), as it's got a nurturing, good-for-the-soul vibe.

**TIME:** 15 MINUTES
**MAKES:** 3½ TABLESPOONS

1 tablespoon nutritional yeast

2 teaspoons onion powder

2 teaspoons paprika

1 teaspoon kosher salt

½ teaspoon dried parsley

¼ teaspoon garlic powder

¼ teaspoon ground turmeric

¼ teaspoon dried dill

¼ teaspoon dried marjoram

In a spice grinder, combine the nutritional yeast, onion powder, paprika, salt, parsley, garlic powder, turmeric, dill, and marjoram. Grind thoroughly into a fine powder. Store in an airtight container in a cool, dark place for up to 3 months.

# cheese sauce

This sauce is as American as apple pie. It evokes childhood nostalgia, and has much to do with the popularity of our Mac and Cheese (page 170) and Grilled Cheese (page 88). Our chef recommends you get creative with it, as there are innumerable applications for its use: for example, in a broccoli-and-cheese bake, as a chip dip, etc.

**AHEAD:** SOAK CASHEWS OVERNIGHT

**TIME:** 20 MINUTES (PLUS SOAKING OVERNIGHT)

**MAKES:** 5 CUPS

1 tablespoon olive oil

¾ cup medium-diced yellow onion

2 garlic cloves, coarsely chopped

2½ cups raw cashews, soaked overnight, then drained

3 cups water

2 tablespoons fresh lemon juice

½ cup nutritional yeast

1 teaspoon kosher salt

½ teaspoon Dijon mustard

½ teaspoon domestic paprika

½ teaspoon dark chili powder

1 In a medium saucepan, heat the olive oil over medium heat. Add the onion and garlic and cook for 5 minutes, stirring often, until the onion is tender and translucent.

2 Carefully transfer the mixture to a high-speed blender and add the cashews, water, lemon juice, nutritional yeast, salt, mustard, paprika, and chili powder. Blend on high speed for about 2 minutes, stopping to scrape down the sides as needed, until completely smooth. Store in an airtight container in the refrigerator for up to 1 week.

# romesco sauce

This robust condiment is Spanish in origin and has historically been used to add pizzazz to otherwise mild dishes. Ours is a red pepper–based sauce, which, in keeping with tradition, utilizes almonds and bread as thickeners. It's earthy, smoky, and rich. We smother our farinata (page 150) in this sauce, but it can also be tossed onto any pasta or used as a dip for veggies.

**TIME:** 45 MINUTES

**MAKES:** 3 CUPS

5 red bell peppers

¼ cup plus 3 tablespoons olive oil

½ cup raw almonds

3 garlic cloves, peeled

2 tablespoons red wine vinegar

1 tablespoon smoked paprika

1 teaspoon kosher salt

**1** Preheat the oven to 500°F.

**2** Place the whole bell peppers on a baking sheet and drizzle them with 3 tablespoons of the olive oil. Roast for 30 to 40 minutes, turning the peppers over twice while roasting, until the skins are completely wrinkled and charred. Transfer the peppers to a medium bowl and immediately cover the bowl tightly with plastic wrap; reduce the oven temperature to 350°F. Set the peppers aside for 30 minutes, or until they are cool enough to handle.

**3** Spread the almonds on a baking sheet. Toast in the oven for about 10 minutes, until the almonds are fragrant. Remove from the oven and set aside.

**4** When the roasted peppers are cool to the touch, peel each pepper and discard the stem and seeds, placing the flesh in a bowl as you go, along with any juices that have collected in the bowl.

**5** Transfer the peppers to a food processor and add the toasted almonds, the remaining ¼ cup olive oil, the garlic, vinegar, paprika, and salt. Process until the sauce is relatively smooth, with some texture from the almonds. Store in an airtight container in the refrigerator for up to 1 week.

# romesco aioli

We make a lot of romesco aioli at Little Pine. It's a versatile sauce we use as a dip for our smashed potatoes (page 136), a base for our Fennel Flatbread Pizza (page 166), and a spread for our Breakfast Sandwiches (page 85). You can likewise keep it in the fridge year-round for veggie-dipping, sammy-spreading, or just licking off a spoon, if you're so inclined.

**TIME:** 10 MINUTES
**MAKES:** 2 CUPS

1 cup Romesco Sauce (page 37)

1 cup vegan mayonnaise

In a small bowl, combine the romesco sauce and mayonnaise. Mix well until fully incorporated. Use immediately or transfer to an airtight container and store in the refrigerator for up to 1 week.

# pesto aioli

I can't imagine a world in which we serve our Broccoli Arancini (page 140) without this dip; the two were just born for each other. (Or made for each other, by our chef, but you get the point.) This sauce is walnut-based, which means it's packed full of nutrients, so I suggest you keep it on hand to jazz up or make healthier sandwiches, vegetable spreads, and the like.

**TIME:** 20 MINUTES
**MAKES:** 1½ CUPS

¼ cup walnut pieces

2 garlic cloves, peeled

½ teaspoon kosher salt

2 tablespoons fresh lemon juice

3 tablespoons water

6 tablespoons olive oil

2 cups packed fresh basil (large stems removed)

1 cup vegan mayonnaise

1  In a food processor, combine the walnuts, garlic, salt, lemon juice, and water. Process until the mixture is as smooth as possible. With the motor running, slowly pour in the olive oil in a steady stream, then slowly add the basil and process until smooth. Be sure not to let the motor get hot or the pesto will turn brown.

2  Transfer the pesto to a small bowl and add the mayonnaise. Stir until fully incorporated. Use immediately or transfer to an airtight container and store in the refrigerator for up to 1 week.

romesco aioli

pesto aioli

kimchi aioli, *page 139*

# pickled red onions

We use these pickled onions on our Breakfast Sandwiches (page 85) as well as in our Charred Broccolini (page 144), but I recommend you keep a jar on hand at all times. They'll add a little oomph to any number of dishes, including but not limited to sandwiches, avocado toast, tacos, and pizza. Making these is also a great way to reduce food waste: if you're using just part of a red onion for another recipe, simply pickle the rest.

**TIME:** 25 MINUTES
**MAKES:** 3 CUPS

1 cup champagne vinegar

1 cup sugar

2 cups water

2 cups thinly sliced red onions

1  In a small saucepan, combine the vinegar, sugar, and water and bring to a boil over medium-high heat, stirring continuously so the sugar does not stick to the bottom of the saucepan, until the sugar has dissolved completely. Remove from the heat.

2  Place the onions in a small bowl and pour the pickling liquid over them. Let cool completely, then transfer to a jar, seal, and store in the refrigerator for up to 1 month.

# chili-smoked almonds

If you want to jazz up a salad or cooked greens, these fancy nuts are a great way to do so. Plus, you get to use a Smoking Gun, which sounds pretty cool . . . as in "Don't bother me, I'm using my Smoking Gun!" You can also serve these as a pre-dinner snack or with cocktails.

**TIME:** 30 MINUTES
**MAKES:** 1 CUP

1 cup raw almonds

1 teaspoon kosher salt

½ teaspoon chili powder

¼ teaspoon cayenne pepper

1  Preheat the oven to 325°F.

2  Place the almonds on a small baking sheet. Toast in the oven for 8 to 10 minutes, until fragrant. Transfer to a bowl. Fill the chamber of a Smoking Gun with hickory chips. Place the tube from the smoker in the bowl and cover the bowl with plastic wrap. Turn the smoker on, light the chips, and fill the bowl with smoke. Turn the smoker off and let the almonds stand until the smoke dissipates.

3  Transfer the almonds to a food processor and add the salt, chili powder, and cayenne. Pulse until the almonds are finely chopped. Store in an airtight container indefinitely.

*I live in Little Pine's backyard, and I steal their nuts whenever I can. Sometimes they're spicy!*
*— Chip the squirrel*

# italian sausage

Our housemade Italian sausage is by no means the easiest recipe in this book, but the payoff is great: it tastes (I'm told) exactly like its mainstream alternative. Make it in big batches and freeze it for future use.

**TIME:** 2 HOURS 30 MINUTES

**MAKES:** 3 SAUSAGES

2½ cups water

1 cup dry bulgur wheat

½ cup olive oil, plus more for greasing

4 cups chopped yellow onions

6 tablespoons minced garlic

6 tablespoons tamari

¼ cup white miso paste

¼ cup peanut butter

3 tablespoons red wine vinegar

1½ tablespoons kosher salt

2 teaspoons freshly ground black pepper

2 teaspoons dried basil

2 teaspoons ground fennel

2 teaspoons dried thyme

1½ teaspoons granulated garlic

1 teaspoon paprika

½ teaspoon red pepper flakes

2 pinches of dried oregano

3 cups vital wheat gluten

**1** In a small saucepan, bring 2 cups of the water to a boil. Place the bulgur in a medium bowl and pour the boiling water over it. Cover the bowl tightly with plastic wrap and let the bulgur steam for 15 minutes, or until fully hydrated. Drain off any excess water.

**2** In a medium skillet, heat the olive oil over medium-high heat. Once heated, add the onions and garlic to the skillet and sauté until soft. (It will seem like a lot of oil, but it adds the right amount of fat to the finished sausage.) Transfer the contents of the pan to a blender and add the remaining ½ cup water, the tamari, miso, peanut butter, vinegar, salt, black pepper, basil, fennel, thyme, granulated garlic, paprika, red pepper flakes, and oregano. Blend until completely smooth. Transfer the mixture to a large bowl. Add the bulgur and mix thoroughly to combine.

**3** Add the vital wheat gluten to the bulgur mixture 1 cup at a time, mixing well and breaking up any clumps. As the mixture begins to come together, you can begin to knead it by hand, but be careful not to overwork it.

**4** Cut three 12-inch square pieces of aluminum foil and grease the foil well with olive oil. When all the vital wheat gluten has been incorporated, separate the sausage mixture into three equal portions. Place one piece on a square of foil, on the side closest to you. Spread the mixture evenly from left to right to form a loaf, leaving 4 inches of foil

RECIPE CONTINUES →

on each side and enough room to roll the mixture over on itself three times. Fold the end of the foil closest to you over the sausage to cover it. Press in to get an even consistency throughout the sausage. Roll the mixture over again, trying your best to press out any air holes or cracks in the sausage (the sausage mixture is very forgiving). Repeat until you reach the end of the foil. Once the sausage is fully wrapped, twist the ends of the foil to tighten the roll. Repeat to form two additional sausages.

5  Fill a large pot with 2 inches of water and top with a steamer basket. Lay the sausages in the steamer and cover (you can cook them one at a time if they don't all fit in the basket). Steam over high heat for 1 hour 30 minutes. Carefully remove the sausages from the steamer basket and place them on a tray to cool for about 1 hour before transferring them to the fridge to cool completely. Store wrapped in the refrigerator for up to 1 week and in the freezer for up to 2 months.

# herbed bread crumbs

Add these into anything that needs a little crunch or added richness—at Little Pine, they feature in our LA-famous Mac and Cheese (page 170) as well as in our Celery Root Cassoulet (page 164). We use gluten-free bread, but you can grab your favorite variety or just whatever's on hand.

**TIME:** 45 MINUTES

**MAKES:** 1 CUP

½ loaf bread of your choice, cut into 1-inch pieces (about 1 cup)

¼ cup olive oil

Leaves from 4 sprigs rosemary, minced

Leaves from 4 sprigs thyme, minced

2 garlic cloves, minced

1 teaspoon kosher salt

1  Preheat the oven to 250°F.

2  In a medium bowl, toss together the bread, olive oil, rosemary, thyme, garlic, and salt. Spread the mixture evenly over a baking sheet. Toast in the oven for about 30 minutes, until golden brown, checking on the bread frequently and stirring. Remove from the oven and let cool.

3  Crumble the bread into a large bowl until reduced to fine crumbs, or pulse in a food processor until the desired size crumbs are achieved.

4  Store in an airtight container at room temperature for up to 1 month.

mac and cheese, *page 170*

# brunch

# bagels

Bagels. In some ways, I think I should just leave this recipe blurb at that: bagels. One word. Simple and round and doughy, almost like onomatopoeia. When I was growing up in and around New York, bagels were as ubiquitous as taxis and pigeons. And before I got sober, my favorite hangover cure was a green smoothie and an onion bagel with vegan olive cream cheese. And sleep. And more sleep. I'm sober now, but I still love bagels. I should probably go back and edit this and just leave it as a one-word reductionist intro. Bagels.

**TIME:** 2 HOURS 10 MINUTES

**MAKES:** 12 BAGELS

**SPONGE**

4 cups unbleached all-purpose flour

1 teaspoon active dry yeast

2½ cups room-temperature water

**DOUGH**

3¾ cups unbleached all-purpose flour

½ teaspoon active dry yeast

1 tablespoon kosher salt

1 tablespoon agave nectar

Neutral oil, such as canola oil, for greasing

1 tablespoon baking soda

Egg Wash (page 17)

Everything Spice (page 34), for topping

1  **MAKE THE SPONGE:** In a large bowl, mix together the flour, yeast, and water. Cover and let stand until doubled in size, about 1 hour.

2  **MAKE THE DOUGH:** Transfer the sponge to the bowl of a stand mixer fitted with the dough hook. Add the flour, yeast, salt, and agave and mix on medium-low speed until the dough is smooth.

3  Line two baking sheets with parchment paper and lightly oil the parchment. Split the dough into 12 equal pieces. Gently shape each piece like a steering wheel, poking a hole in the middle of the dough and stretching it until the hole in the middle is about 1 inch in size. Place the shaped dough on the prepared baking sheets, 6 per sheet. Cover the dough and let rest for 20 minutes.

4  Preheat the oven to 375°F.

5  In a large pot, bring 8 cups of water to a boil over high heat. Carefully add the baking soda, then drop in the bagels and cook for 30 seconds on each side. Return the boiled bagels to the baking sheets and pat them dry, then brush them with egg wash and sprinkle with everything spice.

6  Bake for 20 to 25 minutes, until dark golden brown. Remove from the oven and let cool on the pan completely before serving. Store, covered, at room temperature for up to 2 days.

# banana chocolate walnut muffins

Muffins are fluffy breakfast cupcakes, sans frosting. These have a cinnamon streusel topping, which allows them to still read as a morning meal, albeit on the decadent side (thank you, vegan chocolate chips). I mean, life is hard for lots of people, so if you want cake for breakfast, I hereby offer you a socially acceptable way to live a little. (Plus, even though these muffins are indulgent, they still have the superfood punch of chocolate, walnuts, and bananas.)

**TIME:** 40 MINUTES

**MAKES:** 12 MUFFINS

### MUFFINS

2½ bananas, mashed

¾ cup granulated sugar

6 tablespoons loosely packed light brown sugar

6 tablespoons canola oil

4½ tablespoons water

¾ teaspoon pure vanilla extract

2¼ cups unbleached all-purpose flour

4½ teaspoons Bob's Red Mill Egg Replacer

1 teaspoon baking soda

1 teaspoon baking powder

¾ teaspoon kosher salt

⅛ teaspoon ground cinnamon

⅛ teaspoon ground nutmeg

¾ cup walnuts, chopped

1½ cups vegan dark chocolate chips

### CINNAMON STREUSEL

1¼ cups unbleached all-purpose flour

¾ cup granulated sugar

1 teaspoon ground cinnamon

¾ teaspoon kosher salt

½ cup Hard Butter (page 14), cubed and chilled

1　Preheat the oven to 375°F. Line a standard muffin tin with paper liners.

2　**MAKE THE MUFFINS:** In the bowl of a stand mixer fitted with the paddle attachment, combine the bananas, granulated sugar, brown sugar, oil, water, and vanilla and mix on medium-low speed until combined. Sift the flour, egg replacer, baking soda, baking powder, salt, cinnamon, and nutmeg into the wet ingredients and mix on low speed to incorporate. Using a spatula, gently fold in the walnuts and chocolate chips. Divide the batter evenly among the prepared muffin cups, using about ⅓ cup of the batter per muffin.

3　**MAKE THE STREUSEL:** In the bowl of a stand mixer fitted with the paddle attachment, combine the flour, granulated sugar, cinnamon, and salt. Add the butter and mix on low speed until a dough begins to form.

4　Top each muffin with about 3 tablespoons of the streusel. Bake for 25 minutes, rotating the pan halfway through, until the muffins are golden brown and the tops spring back when touched. Let the muffins cool for 10 minutes before transferring to a wire rack to cool completely. Store, covered, at room temperature for up to 3 days.

# cinnamon walnut shortcakes

What, exactly, makes a cake short? I asked the internet machine, and it turns out that it doesn't so much have to do with height as it does texture: shortcakes are not cakes, per se, but rather sugary biscuits. (The more you know . . .) This recipe offers a cold-weather alternative to shortcake's most famous preparation—strawberries and whipped cream, of course—that can be enjoyed any time of day. I think it'd make an especially perfect addition to your next holiday brunch spread, and none of your dairy-loving relatives will have a clue that it's milk- and butter-free.

**TIME:** 2 HOURS

**MAKES:** 9 SHORTCAKES

## NUT MIXTURE

½ cup walnuts, chopped

1 tablespoon ground cinnamon

1 teaspoon granulated sugar

## DOUGH

2 cups unbleached all-purpose flour

1 cup rolled oats

¾ cup granulated sugar

1 tablespoon baking powder

¼ teaspoon kosher salt

½ cup Hard Butter (page 14), cubed and chilled

¾ cup Cashew Cream (page 18), plus more for brushing

1 tablespoon ground flaxseeds, whisked with 3 tablespoons cold water

1 teaspoon pure vanilla extract

## MAPLE GLAZE

1 cup powdered sugar

¼ cup pure maple syrup

⅛ teaspoon kosher salt

**1** Preheat the oven to 350°F.

**2 MAKE THE NUT MIXTURE:** Place the walnuts on a baking sheet and toast in the oven for 8 to 10 minutes, until golden and fragrant. Remove from the oven and let cool completely. Transfer the walnuts to a small bowl and stir in the cinnamon and granulated sugar. Set aside.

**3** Line a baking sheet with parchment paper.

**4 MAKE THE DOUGH:** In a medium bowl, mix together the flour, oats, granulated sugar, baking powder, and salt. Cut in the cubed butter with your fingers (or a pastry blender) until the butter is broken down to the size of hazelnuts and evenly dispersed throughout the mixture.

**5** In a small bowl, whisk together the cashew cream, flax mixture, and vanilla. Add this mixture to the dry ingredients in two stages, folding it in gently until the dough is combined but still shaggy. Add half the nut mixture, fold the dough in half, and repeat.

**6** Using a 3-ounce scoop, scoop the dough onto the prepared baking sheet, spacing the mounds evenly. Freeze the dough for 1 hour to set.

**7** Preheat the oven to 400°F.

**8** Brush the tops of the shortcakes with cashew cream and bake for 20 to 25 minutes, until golden brown.

**9 MEANWHILE, MAKE THE MAPLE GLAZE:** In a small bowl, whisk together the powdered sugar, maple syrup, and salt until combined.

**10** While the shortcakes are still hot, drizzle them with the maple glaze. Let cool completely before serving. Leftover shortcakes will keep for a few days in an airtight container.

# cinnamon rolls

In 1987, "veganism" usually meant oat groats and soy grits and carob, whereas today it can mean sublime cinnamon rolls. I half expect to wake up and find myself back in 1987 with a bowl of cold soy grits, lamenting that this golden age of veganism was just a dream . . .

**TIME:** 4 HOURS 15 MINUTES

**MAKES:** 12 CINNAMON ROLLS

### DOUGH

8 cups unbleached all-purpose flour

2½ cups unsweetened soy milk

4½ teaspoons kosher salt

¾ cup Hard Butter (page 14), at room temperature

1 cup granulated sugar

1 tablespoon plus 1 teaspoon active dry yeast

### FILLING

2 cups Hard Butter (page 14), at room temperature

4 cups packed light brown sugar

1 cup ground cinnamon

1½ teaspoons kosher salt

1½ teaspoons pure vanilla extract

### CINNAMON ROLL FROSTING

2 cups Hard Butter (page 14), at room temperature

6 cups powdered sugar

½ teaspoon kosher salt

1 teaspoon pure vanilla extract

2 tablespoons unsweetened soy milk

**1  MAKE THE DOUGH:** In the bowl of a stand mixer fitted with a dough hook, combine the flour, soy milk, salt, butter, granulated sugar, and yeast and knead on low speed until a stiff ball of dough forms. Cover the bowl and refrigerate for at least 2 hours and up to 1 week.

**2  MEANWHILE, MAKE THE FILLING:** In the bowl of a stand mixer fitted with the paddle attachment, combine the butter, brown sugar, cinnamon, salt, and vanilla and mix on low speed until thoroughly combined.

**3** Line a baking sheet with parchment paper and lightly oil the parchment. On a floured surface, roll out the dough into an 18 × 14-inch rectangle, positioning one long edge facing you. Spread the filling over the dough and, starting from the edge closest to you, roll up the dough tightly and pinch the seam to seal. Cut the log crosswise into 1½-inch-wide pieces and place them, evenly spaced, on the prepared baking sheet. Cover with a clean kitchen towel and let stand until doubled in size, about 1 hour.

**4** Preheat the oven to 350°F.

**5** Bake the cinnamon rolls for 25 to 30 minutes, until golden brown.

**6  MEANWHILE, MAKE THE CINNAMON ROLL FROSTING:** In the bowl of a stand mixer fitted with the paddle attachment, combine the butter, powdered sugar, salt, and vanilla and mix on low speed until combined. With the mixer on low speed, pour in the soy milk and mix until creamy.

**7** While the cinnamon rolls are still warm, top each with about ¼ cup of the frosting. Serve immediately. Store in an airtight container at room temperature for up to 2 days or in the refrigerator for up to 3 days. To reheat, place on a foil-covered baking tray and heat at 350°F for 10 minutes.

# orange cranberry scones

Cranberries are an overlooked fruit, but they're exceptionally high in antioxidants, fiber, and vitamin C while being relatively low in sugar. Since they tend to skew wintery, especially in combination with orange flavors, this scone recipe just screams "holiday" to me. Prep them for breakfast when the whole family is in town or, if you're like me and basically have no family, share them with your friends, both real and imaginary (no judgment).

**TIME:** 1 HOUR
**MAKES:** 8 SCONES

4 cups unbleached all-purpose flour

½ cup granulated sugar

2½ teaspoons baking powder

½ teaspoon baking soda

1 teaspoon kosher salt

1½ cups unsweetened dried cranberries

1 tablespoon orange zest

1 cup Hard Butter (page 14), cubed and chilled

1⅓ cups Cashew Cream (page 18), plus more for brushing

Turbinado sugar, for topping

**1** In a large bowl, mix together the flour, granulated sugar, baking powder, baking soda, salt, cranberries, and orange zest. Cut in the cubed butter with your fingers (or a pastry blender) until the butter is broken down into pieces the size of hazelnuts and evenly dispersed.

**2** Stir in the cashew cream a little at a time until the dough is just combined; do not overmix.

**3** Preheat the oven to 400°F. Line a baking sheet with parchment paper.

**4** Turn out the dough onto a floured surface and roll it into a 1-inch-thick round. Cut the round into 8 equal triangles and place them on the prepared baking sheet, spacing them evenly. Freeze the scones for 15 minutes to set before baking.

**5** Brush the tops of the scones with cashew cream and sprinkle with turbinado sugar. Bake for 20 to 23 minutes, until golden brown. Store in an airtight container at room temperature for up to 3 days.

# chocolate-glazed old-fashioned donuts

Let's be honest: one of the (many) great things about plant-based eating is that you almost always feel like you're being healthy . . . even when cake-for-breakfast is involved. I regularly subscribe to that line of magical thinking, particularly when it comes to these chocolate-glazed beauties, because life is too short to be lived without donuts. Plus, while I'm eating one (or four) of these donuts, I can tell myself that dark chocolate is totally an antioxidant.

**TIME:** 3 HOURS 30 MINUTES

**MAKES:** ABOUT 12 DONUTS

## DOUGH

4¼ cups unbleached all-purpose flour, plus more for dusting

2 cups sugar

2 teaspoons baking powder

½ teaspoon baking soda

1 teaspoon kosher salt

1½ cups unsweetened soy milk, at room temperature

2 tablespoons Hard Butter (page 14), melted

2 teaspoons pure vanilla extract

## CHOCOLATE GLAZE

1 cup vegan dark chocolate chips

¼ cup Hard Butter (page 14)

2 tablespoons agave nectar

4 teaspoons water

—

Sunflower oil, for frying

**1  MAKE THE DOUGH:** In the bowl of a stand mixer fitted with the paddle attachment, combine the flour, sugar, baking powder, baking soda, and salt. In a liquid measuring cup, whisk together the milk, melted butter, and vanilla. With the mixer running on low speed, pour in the wet ingredients and mix until the dough comes together; it will be very sticky.

**2**  Turn the dough out onto a piece of parchment paper sprinkled generously with flour. Flour the top of the dough and place another piece of parchment paper on top. Roll out the dough into a rectangle about ½ inch thick. Slide the dough, still between the sheets of parchment, onto a baking sheet or tray and freeze for 2 hours.

**3  MEANWHILE, MAKE THE CHOCOLATE GLAZE:** In a medium pot, combine the chocolate chips, butter, agave, and water and heat over medium-low heat, stirring gently, until completely melted and smooth. Remove from the heat and set aside until ready to use.

**4**  Remove the dough from the freezer. Discard the top sheet of parchment and, using a floured donut cutter, cut out donuts. If desired, gather the

RECIPE CONTINUES ➔

scraps of dough, roll them out between two pieces of parchment, freeze for 2 hours, and cut out more donuts; discard any scraps that remain.

5   Fill a large Dutch oven with 2 inches of sunflower oil and heat over medium heat to 350°F. Line a baking sheet with paper towels and set it nearby.

6   With a paring knife, score a square into the top of each donut. (The scoring will give the old-fashioned donuts their iconic cracked texture.) Place up to 3 donuts at a time in the hot oil and fry for 1 to 1½ minutes, until golden on the bottom, then flip with tongs and fry for another 1 to 1½ minutes, until equally golden on the second side. Remove the donuts from the oil and place them on the paper towel–lined baking sheet to drain and cool slightly. Repeat to fry the remaining donuts.

7   Carefully dip the tops of the donuts into the chocolate glaze and place them on a wire rack to set for about 3 minutes before serving. These are best eaten the same day.

FRIENDS OF LITTLE PINE

ROTINI @MYVEGANPIG

*I eat like a pig at Little Pine. I love their roasted potatoes at brunch or at any other time of day. Little Pine makes me feel safe and surrounded by friends who love animals. Congratulations, Little Pine, on this cookbook, and thank you for sharing your yummy recipes and spreading love for animals.*

# the perfect danish

Every Sunday when I was growing up, my grandparents took me to Noroton Presbyterian Church, where my grandfather taught Sunday school and my grandmother edited the newsletter. I don't remember much about the actual church services (except that the pastor wore golf clothes under his black robes), but I do remember going with my grandparents to Jutland Bakery afterward to buy Danishes. Our Little Pine Danishes are, dare I say it, as indulgent as the ones I ate as a child on those Sundays. To me, the perfect Danish—like this one—is as much about the complementary textures as it is about the fruit and sweetness.

**TIME:** 2 HOURS 30 MINUTES

**MAKES:** 16 DANISHES

Flour, for dusting

1 pack Laminated Dough (page 68)

Egg Wash (page 17)

1 cup Cashew Cream Cheese (page 18)

Fresh fruit of choice

**GLAZE**

1 cup powdered sugar

2 tablespoons unsweetened soy milk

¼ teaspoon pure vanilla extract

—

Simple Syrup (page 27), for brushing

**1** Line two baking sheets with parchment paper. On a floured surface, roll out the laminated dough into a 16-inch square, then cut it into sixteen 4-inch squares. Brush the center of each piece with egg wash. Fold two opposite corners of the dough into the center and press firmly to secure, creating a diamond shape. Spoon 1 tablespoon of the cream cheese onto the center of each piece and top it with fruit. Place the Danishes on the prepared baking sheets as you go. Once you have formed all the Danishes, cover them with a clean kitchen towel and set aside in a warm area to proof for 1 hour 30 minutes.

**2** Preheat the oven to 400°F.

**3** Brush the edges of the Danishes with egg wash and bake for 20 to 25 minutes, rotating the pans halfway through, until golden brown.

**4** **MEANWHILE, MAKE THE GLAZE:** In a small bowl, whisk together the powdered sugar, soy milk, and vanilla until no lumps remain.

**5** Immediately after removing the Danishes from the oven, brush them with simple syrup. Let cool completely, then drizzle with the glaze. Store, covered, at room temperature for up to 2 days.

# croissants

I bet you didn't open this book expecting to find a self-involved sob story, but here it is: when I lived in France in the late '80s, I was unable to eat croissants because they are typically not vegan. Tragic, but now I have our Little Pine croissants, which are not only vegan but amazing (and I can say that with objectivity, as I had nothing to do with formulating the recipe—it involves a level of pastry-kitchen magic of which I can only dream). Once you make your own perfect croissant, you can do anything with it: eat it with jam or jelly, cover it with chocolate, or even just enjoy it plain while listening to old Jacques Brel records.

**TIME:** 3 HOURS
**MAKES:** 6 CROISSANTS

Flour, for dusting

1 pack Laminated Dough (recipe follows)

Egg Wash (page 17)

Flaky sea salt, such as Maldon, for garnish

1  Line a baking sheet with parchment paper. On a floured surface, roll out the laminated dough into a 12-inch square. Cut the square into three 4-inch-wide strips, then cut the strips in half diagonally so you have 6 triangular pieces of dough total.

2  To form the croissants, begin by brushing the narrow tips of each triangle of dough with egg wash. Cut a ½-inch-long slit in the center of the wide end of the triangle and roll up the dough from the wide end to the narrow end. Place each croissant on the prepared baking sheet as you form them and cover with a clean kitchen towel. Once you have finished rolling all six croissants, set the baking sheet in a warm area to proof for 2 hours.

3  Preheat the oven to 400°F.

4  Brush the croissants with egg wash and sprinkle with flaky salt. Bake for 25 to 30 minutes, rotating the pan halfway through, until golden brown. Store, covered, at room temperature for up to 2 days.

RECIPE CONTINUES ➜

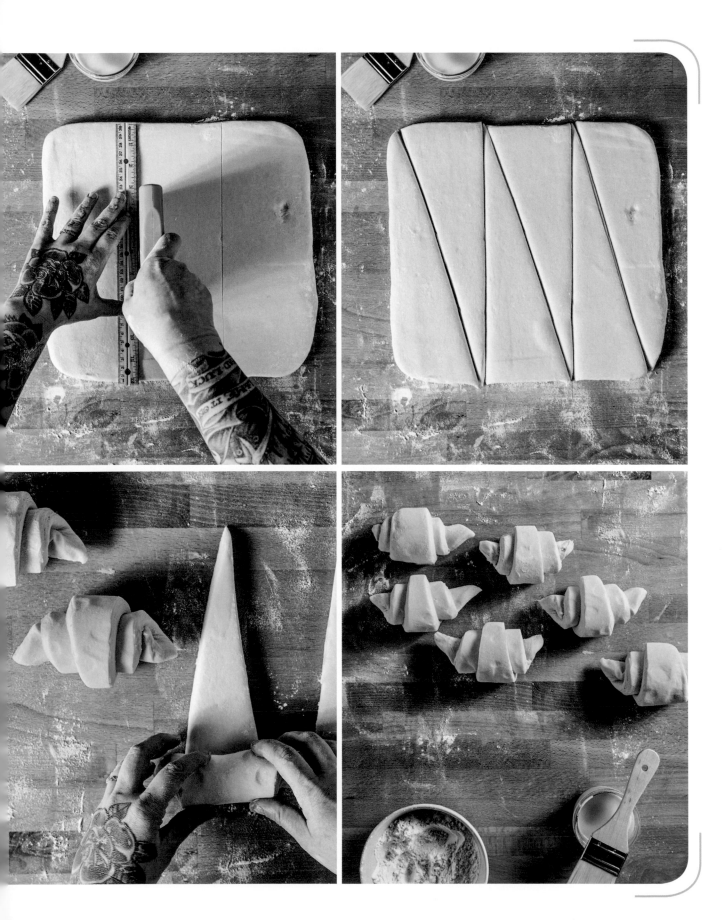

# laminated dough

Dough lamination is a culinary technique that involves repeated folding and rolling. This creates layers of buttery dough that provide for flaky pastry perfection.

**TIME:** 3 HOURS
30 MINUTES

**MAKES:** 12 CROISSANTS
OR 32 DANISHES

3 cups unsweetened
soy milk

1½ tablespoons
active dry yeast

1 teaspoon kosher salt

3 tablespoons sugar

½ cup plus 1 tablespoon
Hard Butter (page 14),
at room temperature

9⅓ cups unbleached
all-purpose flour

3 cups (6 sticks)
store-bought vegan butter,
at room temperature

1  In the bowl of a stand mixer, combine the milk, yeast, salt, sugar, and hard butter. Use a whisk to stir this mixture together and break up any large pieces of butter. Add the flour and, with a dough hook fitted to your mixer, mix on low speed until a cohesive dough forms. Loosely wrap the dough in plastic wrap and refrigerate for 1 hour 30 minutes.

2  Line a baking sheet with parchment paper. On a floured surface, roll out your dough into a 16 × 24-inch rectangle. Spread the butter evenly over two-thirds of the dough. Fold the uncovered third of the dough over the center third of the dough, and then fold the remaining third of the dough over the previous fold. Transfer the dough to the prepared baking sheet, cover with plastic wrap, and refrigerate for 20 minutes.

3  Unwrap the dough and set it on a floured surface with the seam side up and one long side facing you. Roll out once again into a 16 × 24-inch rectangle and repeat the same folds as earlier. Transfer the dough to the same baking sheet, cover with plastic wrap, and refrigerate for 20 minutes.

4  Repeat the previous step once more, stopping after you've folded the dough. Use a sharp knife to carefully trim both ends of the dough so the edges are clean. Cut the dough in half to create two equal squares. Wrap each pack of dough tightly in plastic wrap and refrigerate until ready to use, or for up to 7 days. Any unused dough may be frozen for up to 1 month. Defrost in the refrigerator overnight before using.

# berry granola bowls

This might sound like some old-school hippie vegan breakfast item, but to be clear, it absolutely isn't . . . those three words—"berry," "granola," and "bowl"— are woefully misleading, as this is a next-level breakfast/brunch indulgence. It pairs protein-packed hemp seed granola with berries (read: nature's candy) and our incredibly decadent coconut whipped cream to *chef's kiss* effect.

**TIME:** 10 MINUTES

**SERVES:** 4

2 cups Coconut Whipped Cream (page 22)

4 cups Hemp Seed Granola (page 33)

1 apple, cored and cut into ¼-inch-thick slices

2 cups fresh berries

Portion ½ cup of the coconut whipped cream into each of four bowls and top each bowl with 1 cup of the granola. Garnish with the apple slices and fresh berries.

# strawberry pop-tarts

Once upon a time, lost in the wilds of suburban Connecticut, I was a junk food—devouring teenage boy, and I loved Pop-Tarts. Not to malign the original, but while this vegan version isn't exactly a salad, it's still a considerable upgrade from the highly processed, nonvegan strawberry filling. Little Pine regulars come in just to satisfy their cravings for this housemade Pop-Tart redux. It's perfect for serving to teenagers, or just the nostalgic teenager inside you.

**TIME:** 4 HOURS
30 MINUTES
(INCLUDES CHILLING)

**MAKES:** 12 PASTRIES

### PASTRY DOUGH

4¾ cups unbleached all-purpose flour, plus more for dusting

1½ teaspoons granulated sugar

1½ teaspoons kosher salt

2 cups Hard Butter (page 14), cubed and chilled

½ cup cold water

### GLAZE

2 cups powdered sugar

3 tablespoons unsweetened soy milk

½ teaspoon pure vanilla extract

### FILLING AND ASSEMBLY

Egg Wash (page 17)

¾ cup Strawberry Jam (page 30)

1 cup turbinado sugar

1 ounce freeze-dried strawberries, lightly crushed, for garnish

**1 MAKE THE PASTRY DOUGH:** In the bowl of a stand mixer fitted with the paddle attachment, mix together the flour, granulated sugar, and salt. With the mixer on low speed, add the butter and mix until it breaks down into pieces the size of hazelnuts. Slowly stream in the water and mix until the dough is just combined; do not overmix.

**2** On a floured surface, pat the dough into a rectangle with one long side facing you. Fold the right third of the dough over the center third of the dough, then fold the remaining third of the dough over the center.

**3** Split the dough in half horizontally, pat each half of the dough into a square, and wrap each square tightly in plastic wrap. Refrigerate for at least 2 hours.

**4 MAKE THE GLAZE:** In a medium bowl, whisk together the powdered sugar, soy milk, and vanilla in a medium bowl until completely smooth. Cover and set aside until ready to use.

**5 ASSEMBLE THE PASTRIES:** Remove one pack of the pastry dough from the refrigerator. Roll the dough between two lightly floured sheets of parchment paper into a 12 × 16-inch rectangle about ⅛ inch thick. Cut out twelve 3 × 4-inch rectangles. Place the cut rectangles in an even layer on a baking

RECIPE CONTINUES ➜

sheet and place in the freezer for about 10 minutes, until the dough is chilled enough to handle easily. Repeat with the remaining dough.

**6** Preheat the oven to 375°F.

**7** On a baking sheet or on the counter, lay out 12 pieces of the dough and brush them with the egg wash. Scoop 1 tablespoon of the strawberry jam into the center of each piece, being mindful to keep the jam from spreading to the edges of the pastry. Place a second rectangle of dough on top of each jam-filled rectangle and sandwich them together. Use a floured fork to crimp the sides of each pastry. Carefully poke the tops of the pastries in several spots to allow them to vent steam while baking. Freeze the pastries for 20 minutes before baking.

**8** Brush the tops of the pastries with egg wash and sprinkle them with turbinado sugar. Bake for 30 to 40 minutes, rotating the pan halfway through the baking time, until the pastry is golden and the jam is bubbling. Remove from the oven and let cool completely.

**9** Drizzle the cooled pastries with the glaze and finish with a sprinkle of freeze-dried strawberries. Store, covered, in an airtight container in the refrigerator for up to 1 week.

# chocolate hazelnut crepes

This is a classic, fan-favorite crepe evolved to include a candied hazelnut topping and finished with a squeeze of fresh orange juice. In short, it's delicious, indulgent, and rather sweetly nostalgic.

**TIME:** 50 MINUTES

**MAKES:** 6 TO 8 CREPES

### CHOCOLATE HAZELNUT SPREAD

1½ cups blanched hazelnuts, toasted

¼ cup coconut oil, melted

¾ cup powdered sugar

¼ cup unsweetened cocoa powder

¾ teaspoon pure vanilla extract

½ teaspoon kosher salt

½ cup cold water

### CANDIED HAZELNUTS

¼ plus 2 tablespoons granulated sugar

4½ teaspoons water

½ cup blanched hazelnuts, toasted

⅛ teaspoon kosher salt

### SWEET CREPE BATTER

1½ cups unsweetened almond milk

1 cup unbleached all-purpose flour

2 tablespoons Bob's Red Mill Egg Replacer

1¼ teaspoons water

1 tablespoon sunflower oil, plus more for brushing

### FOR SERVING

1 orange, halved and then quartered, for serving

Powdered sugar, for garnish

**1  MAKE THE CHOCOLATE HAZELNUT SPREAD:** In a food processor, combine the toasted hazelnuts, coconut oil, powdered sugar, cocoa powder, vanilla, and salt and process until the mixture is as smooth as you can get it. With the motor running, slowly stream in the water until the mixture is emulsified and smooth. Transfer the spread to an airtight container and keep refrigerated until ready to use, or for up to 4 weeks.

**2  MAKE THE CANDIED HAZELNUTS:** Line a baking sheet with parchment paper. In a small saucepan, combine the granulated sugar and water and heat over high heat, swirling the pan until the sugar dissolves. Bring the sugar mixture to a simmer and cook, swirling the pan occasionally, until it turns a medium amber color. Add the toasted hazelnuts and salt and gently stir until the hazelnuts are coated. Remove the pan from the heat and pour the candied hazelnuts onto the prepared baking sheet in an even layer. Let cool, then transfer to a food processor and pulse until broken into medium pieces. Set aside.

**3  MAKE THE SWEET CREPE BATTER:** In a medium bowl, whisk together the milk, flour, egg replacer, water, and oil until combined and no lumps remain.

**4**  Brush a medium nonstick skillet with sunflower oil and heat over medium-low heat. Use a 4-ounce ladle or scoop to pour the crepe batter into the skillet. Swirl the batter to evenly coat the pan. Cook for about 2 minutes, until lightly browned, then flip and cook for another 2 minutes, until lightly browned on the second side. Transfer the crepe to a plate and repeat with additional oil and the remaining batter.

**5**  Spread ⅓ cup of the chocolate hazelnut spread evenly over half of each crepe. Fold the crepe in half twice to form a triangle shape and place it on a large plate. Repeat with the remaining crepes. Squeeze the juice from one orange segment over each crepe and finish with a sprinkle of the candied hazelnuts and a dusting of powdered sugar.

# strawberry crepes

To state the obvious, crepes make me think of France. I lived in France for a while in the '80s, and I still have to hand it to the French for coming up with delicious food that is as nice to say as it is to eat. This crepe is reasonably virtuous in that it features fresh strawberries, which are antioxidant-rich and brimming with vitamin C. We top it with our Silver Lake–famous coconut whipped cream, but I think you could add a dripping of Fudge Sauce (page 25) if you're among those who think chocolate for breakfast is the entire reason for life.

**TIME:** 1 HOUR 15 MINUTES
**MAKES:** 6 TO 8 CREPES

1 pound fresh strawberries, hulled and quartered

¼ cup sugar

Sunflower oil, for brushing the pan

1 recipe Sweet Crepe batter (see page 73)

¾ cup Coconut Whipped Cream (page 22)

Edible flowers, for garnish (optional)

1  In a medium bowl, toss the strawberries with the sugar. Let stand for 45 minutes, stirring occasionally, until the strawberries release their juices. Set aside 2 tablespoons of the strawberry juice in a small bowl for garnish.

2  Brush a nonstick medium skillet with oil and heat over medium-low heat. Use a 4-ounce ladle or scoop to pour the crepe batter into the skillet. Immediately swirl the batter around to evenly coat the pan. Cook for about 2 minutes, until the crepe is lightly browned on the bottom, then flip and cook for another 2 minutes, until lightly browned on the second side. Transfer the crepe to a plate and repeat with additional oil and the remaining batter.

3  Use ⅓ cup of strawberry filling per crepe. Place half of the filling (a scant 3 tablespoons) in the center of a crepe. Fold the crepe in half twice to form a triangle shape and place it on a large plate. Place a few dollops of the coconut whipped cream on the crepe and top with the remaining strawberry filling, a drizzle of the reserved strawberry liquid, and a sprinkle of edible flowers. Repeat to fill and plate the remaining crepes, and serve.

strawberry crepes

chocolate hazelnut crepes, *page 73*

# french toast

What can I say about French toast? It's fried bread covered in powdered sugar, or "nom, nom, nom." At the restaurant, we serve it topped with fresh berries to give the illusion of virtue, and I highly recommend you do the same because antioxidants are a modern human's best friend. While I don't have children (largely due to overpopulation and attachment issues), my friends' kids happily gobble these up when they brunch at Little Pine. That they're quick and easy to make is always a bonus for the home chef with multiple mouths to feed on a not-so-lazy Sunday and/or a middle-aged, animal-loving musician hungry after a hike.

**TIME:** 30 MINUTES

**MAKES:** 8 PIECES

4½ teaspoons cornstarch

2 tablespoons plus
2 teaspoons granulated sugar

4½ teaspoons water

¾ cup unsweetened soy milk

1 vanilla bean, split lengthwise and seeds scraped out

1 tablespoon Hard Butter (page 14), melted

4 to 5 tablespoons neutral oil, such as canola oil, for greasing

8 thick-cut slices white bread

¼ cup Maple Butter (page 14)

Fresh berries, for serving

Powdered sugar, for garnish

**1** In a medium bowl, whisk together the cornstarch and granulated sugar. While whisking, slowly stream in the water and soy milk. Add the vanilla seeds. Stream in the melted butter and whisk vigorously until combined.

**2** Lightly oil a large skillet or griddle and heat over medium heat. Dip each slice of bread in the custard mixture to coat, without soaking the bread. Transfer the coated bread to the skillet and fry until golden brown on the bottom, about 2 to 3 minutes, and then flip to cook the other side until golden brown as well. Remove the French toast from the pan and set aside on a plate while you finish the remaining slices.

**3** Slather each piece of French toast with maple butter and top with fresh berries. Dust with powdered sugar and serve.

# lemon poppy seed pancakes

In coming up with menu items, one of my favorite things to do is take fairly conventional elements and combine them in ways that are actually synergistic. The key here is balance, with the subtle tart of the citrus balancing the equally subtle crunch of the poppy seeds and then, of course, the egregiously unsubtle dollop of whipped cream crowning the whole delicious pile. Berries are technically optional, but then again, are they? I'm not sure you're living your best life if you omit them. Personally, I like to partner my pancakes with a side of tempeh bacon because it reminds me of visiting cheap waffle houses with my mom when I was a kid. Add a tofu scramble to experience the full effect of a you-know-what-slam breakfast.

**TIME:** 45 MINUTES

**MAKES:** ABOUT 8 PANCAKES

2 cups unbleached all-purpose flour

¼ cup sugar

2 tablespoons poppy seeds

1½ tablespoons Bob's Red Mill Egg Replacer

1 tablespoon baking powder

1¼ teaspoons kosher salt

1 cup plus 2 tablespoons unsweetened soy milk

¾ cup fresh lemon juice (from 3 to 4 lemons)

1½ teaspoons pure vanilla extract

2 tablespoons plus 1½ teaspoons Hard Butter (page 14), melted

Vegan butter or neutral oil, for greasing

Coconut Whipped Cream (page 22), for serving

Fresh berries, for serving

Powdered sugar, for serving

Maple syrup, for serving

1  In a medium bowl, whisk together the flour, sugar, poppy seeds, egg replacer, baking powder, and salt.

2  In a small bowl, combine the soy milk, lemon juice, and vanilla. Add the wet mixture to the dry ingredients and whisk until any lumps are gone. Whisk in the melted butter until the batter is very smooth.

3  Heat a griddle over medium heat for about 10 minutes and grease the surface with a small amount of butter. Use a ⅓-cup measure to scoop the batter onto the griddle. Cook the pancakes until bubbles start to form on top and the edges begin to turn golden brown, about 2 to 3 minutes, and then flip and cook until the second side is evenly browned. Transfer the pancakes to a plate and repeat to cook the remaining batter.

4  Finish the pancakes with a dollop of coconut whipped cream, some fresh berries, powdered sugar, and maple syrup.

# pumpkin pancakes

Blueberry pancakes are one of my favorite breakfast foods, but when blueberries go out of season, sometimes I'll swap them out for pumpkin. The most famous of winter squashes, pumpkin is similar to other superfoods in that it's exceptionally rich in vitamin A, potassium, and fiber. I don't have a real job, and I like my mornings slow, but since mornings are a harried time for many, it helps that this recipe is simple and relatively expedient. Serve with our housemade maple butter and your favorite vegan syrup (yes, many varieties are *not* vegan, so beware!).

**TIME:** 30 MINUTES

**MAKES:** ABOUT 8 PANCAKES

½ cup plus 2 tablespoons pumpkin puree

¾ cup unsweetened almond milk

½ cup water

3 tablespoons sunflower oil, plus more for greasing

1 teaspoon pure vanilla extract

1¼ cups unbleached all-purpose flour

½ cup sugar

4 teaspoons Bob's Red Mill Egg Replacer

1¼ teaspoons baking powder

1¼ teaspoons kosher salt

½ teaspoon ground cinnamon

½ teaspoon ground nutmeg

⅛ teaspoon ground cloves

Coconut Whipped Cream (page 22), for serving

Fresh berries, for serving

**1** In a large bowl, whisk together the pumpkin, milk, water, oil, and vanilla.

**2** In a medium bowl, sift together the flour, sugar, egg replacer, baking powder, salt, cinnamon, nutmeg, and cloves. Add the dry ingredients to the wet ingredients and whisk together until combined.

**3** Heat a griddle or nonstick skillet over medium heat for about 5 minutes and grease the surface with a small amount of oil. Use a ⅓-cup measure to scoop the batter onto the griddle. Using a spatula, gently pat down the batter slightly to form a round pancake. Cook the pancakes until the edges begin to firm up and turn golden brown, about 2 minutes, then flip and cook until the second side is evenly browned. Transfer the pancakes to a plate and repeat with the remaining batter. Serve with coconut whipped cream and fresh berries.

# biscuits and gravy

My friend Marty grew up in Texas and is very much not a vegan. After Little Pine opened, he joined me for brunch one day and I served him these biscuits and gravy. I looked at him, worried that he was going to storm out of the restaurant, but he surprised me and said, "I'm not a vegan, but dude, these are really good." The gravy is savory, sausage-y perfection, and it doesn't hurt, either, that our pastry chef is a magician; these flaky biscuits may help you break free of your butter codependency forever.

**TIME:** 1 HOUR 30 MINUTES

**SERVES:** 4 TO 6
(MAKES 12 BISCUITS)

1 cup refined coconut oil, melted

Nonstick cooking spray

5 cups unbleached all-purpose flour, plus more for dusting

2 tablespoons plus 2 teaspoons baking powder

2 tablespoons sugar

5 teaspoons kosher salt

2⅓ cups Cashew Cream (page 18), plus more for brushing

Gravy (recipe follows), for serving

1 tablespoon chopped fresh chives, for garnish

## biscuits

1   Line a rimmed baking sheet with aluminum foil, covering the edges. Pour the melted coconut oil onto the prepared pan and freeze for about 20 minutes, until completely solidified. Once solid, remove the coconut oil from the baking sheet and chop it into fine pieces. Return the chopped coconut oil to the freezer to prevent it from softening or melting.

2   Preheat the oven to 350°F. Line two baking sheets with parchment paper and lightly oil the parchment with cooking spray.

3   In a large bowl, whisk together the flour, baking powder, sugar, and salt. Toss the chopped coconut oil into the dry ingredients until it is evenly dispersed. Create a well in the center of the mixture and pour in the cashew cream. Carefully mix with your hands until you create a lumpy yet well-mixed dough with no dry spots of flour.

4   Turn the dough out onto a very well-floured surface and roll it out into a 1-inch-thick rectangle. Fold the right one-third of the dough over the middle one-third of the dough and the left one-third of dough over the first fold. Rotate the dough so that one long side is facing you, roll it out to a

RECIPE CONTINUES ➜

1-inch thickness, and repeat the folds once more. Rotate the dough again so one long side is facing you and roll it out to a 1-inch thickness a final time.

5   Using a 3-inch round cutter, cut biscuits from the dough, pressing straight down into the dough before twisting slightly to release the round. Place the biscuits on the prepared baking sheets, leaving 1 inch between each biscuit. Gently press the dough scraps together to form a ball, roll out to a 1-inch thickness, and continue to cut out biscuits.

6   Brush the tops of the biscuits with cashew cream. Bake for 20 to 25 minutes, until golden brown. Store in an airtight container in the refrigerator for up to 3 days.

7   Cut the biscuits in half, set them on a baking sheet, and place them in the oven for 5 to 6 minutes, until warm. Remove the biscuits from the oven and transfer to a serving plate. Cover with the gravy, garnish with the chives, and serve.

# gravy

**TIME:** 35 MINUTES

**MAKES:** 4 CUPS

1 tablespoon olive oil

2 cups finely chopped Italian Sausage (page 45)

½ small onion, cut into small dice

2 garlic cloves, minced

3½ cups Cashew Cream (page 18)

1 teaspoon kosher salt, plus more if needed

1 teaspoon freshly ground black pepper, plus more if needed

1   Preheat the oven to 350°F.

2   In a medium saucepan, warm the olive oil over high heat. Reduce the heat to medium and add the sausage. Cook, stirring continuously, until crispy and browned. Add the onion and garlic and cook, stirring for about 5 minutes, until the onion is translucent.

3   Add cashew cream, salt, and pepper. Cook, stirring, for 10 to 15 minutes, until the gravy has thickened. Taste to check the seasoning and add more salt and pepper if needed. Keep warm until you are ready to serve.

# breakfast sandwiches

Before I became a vegan thirty-four years ago, I loved junk "food" like Egg McMuffins. Now, some mornings nothing sounds better than a stacked vegan sausage-and-egg (read: tofu) sammy. What I really love about this version is that, unlike its less virtuous traditional counterparts, you won't crash out (physically or ethically) after eating it—you might even get a little help in regulating your blood sugar levels from the bulgur wheat used to make the sausage. Plus, we top our sandwich with avocado, a healthy/indulgent LA-inspired addition, though you can stuff yours with anything your heart desires.

**TIME:** 3 HOURS 30 MINUTES (INCLUDES TIME TO COOK SAUSAGE)

**SERVES:** 4

### TOFU EGG

One 12-ounce block firm tofu, drained

1 heaping tablespoon nutritional yeast

½ teaspoon onion powder

½ teaspoon garlic powder

½ teaspoon kala namak (black salt)

¼ teaspoon ground turmeric

### SANDWICHES

8 slices sourdough bread

1 cup Romesco Aioli (page 38)

2 avocados

¼ red onion, thinly sliced

1 Italian Sausage (page 45), cut lengthwise into roughly ½-inch-thick slices (about 2½ inches long)

2 tablespoons olive oil, for frying

**1  MAKE THE TOFU EGG:** Line a plate with a layer of paper towels. Place the block of tofu on the paper towels and place another layer of paper towels on top of the tofu. Put a plate or a cutting board on top of the paper towels and then weigh it down with something heavy like a book. Press the tofu for 30 minutes, then transfer it to a cutting board and cut it into roughly ½-inch-thick slices. (You will need at least 4 pieces; you should be able to get 6 pieces out of each block.)

**2**  In a medium bowl, whisk together the nutritional yeast, onion powder, garlic powder, kala namak, and turmeric. Gently toss the tofu slices in the spice mixture to coat all sides thoroughly; set aside on a large plate.

**3  MAKE THE SANDWICHES:** Lay the slices of bread out on your work surface and liberally spread the aioli over each slice. Halve and pit the avocados. Using a spoon, scoop the flesh from each avocado half in one piece and place it facedown on a cutting board. Thinly slice the avocado halves lengthwise. Evenly distribute the avocado over four slices of the bread. Evenly distribute the onion over the remaining four slices.

**RECIPE CONTINUES ➜**

**4** Preheat a panini press. In a medium skillet, heat about 1 tablespoon of the olive oil over medium heat. Fry the tofu and sausage for 3 to 5 minutes on each side, until golden brown. Add more olive oil if the pan becomes dry.

**5** Transfer one piece of tofu and one piece of sausage to each onion-topped slice of bread. Carefully place an avocado-topped slice of bread on top to close the sandwiches. Transfer the sandwiches to the panini press and press down gently. Cook the sandwiches, in batches, for 5 to 7 minutes, until the bread is crisp. Cut each sandwich in half and serve.

FRIENDS OF LITTLE PINE

BAGUETTE THE OPOSSUM
@ITSMESESAME

*Little Pine feels like my family but with incredible cooking skills. They make the best food I've ever had in my life! When I want my friends and family to know how much I love and appreciate them, I take them to Little Pine for stuffed shells and fancy s'mores.*

# grilled cheese and tomato soup

Not to sound too pretentious, but this sandwich is Proustian for me—every time I bite into one, I'm sent back to winter in Connecticut when I was seven years old, eating grilled cheese at my grandmother's kitchen counter while watching robins and blue jays fight over the bird fountain. This is one of those dishes nonvegans take for granted, and I included it on the Little Pine menu because I wanted Proustian nostalgia for vegans, too. It wasn't easy, but I think we succeeded in replicating the stretchy, gooey deliciousness people have come to know and love in grilled cheese. We then pair it with a warming, dippable tomato soup deceptively rich in an array of veggies designed to balance out the sandwich's childlike indulgence.

**TIME:** 1 HOUR 45 MINUTES

**SERVES:** 4

## TOMATO SOUP

2 tablespoons olive oil, plus more for drizzling

5 garlic cloves, minced

½ cup medium-diced yellow onion

½ cup medium-diced carrots

½ red bell pepper, chopped

Two 28-ounce cans crushed San Marzano tomatoes

½ cup chopped cauliflower florets

2 teaspoons dried basil

½ teaspoon dried oregano

1 teaspoon kosher salt, plus more if needed

Pinch of red pepper flakes

10 fresh basil leaves, plus more for garnish

## GRILLED CHEESE

8 slices Texas toast or your favorite sandwich bread

¼ cup Romesco Aioli (page 38)

¼ cup Cheese Sauce (page 36)

½ cup shredded vegan parmesan

¼ cup Garlic Butter (page 17), melted

**1  MAKE THE TOMATO SOUP:** In a medium pot, heat the olive oil over medium heat. Add the garlic, onion, and carrots and sauté for 3 to 5 minutes, until the onion is translucent. Add the bell pepper and cook for 2 minutes more. Add the tomatoes, cauliflower, dried basil, oregano, salt, and red pepper flakes and bring the mixture to a boil. Reduce the heat to maintain a simmer, cover, and cook for 25 minutes.

**2**  Carefully transfer the soup to a blender and add the fresh basil. Blend until smooth. Taste and adjust the seasoning if needed. Keep warm until ready to serve.

**3  MEANWHILE, MAKE THE GRILLED CHEESE:** Preheat a panini press if you have one (or heat a cast-iron skillet over medium-high heat). Lay the slices of bread out on a clean work surface. Spread the

RECIPE CONTINUES →

# pan bagnat

In 2002 I opened a restaurant on Rivington Street, on the Lower East Side of Manhattan, called Teany. My go-to staple on the Teany menu was our pan bagnat, so it stood to reason that when Little Pine opened, we'd come up with our LA version of this lovely little sandwich. Unlike many a soggy sammy, this one gets better as it sits and soaks up the juice of its tomato confit, so pack it ahead for a picnic brunch, if you like.

**TIME:** 2 HOURS 30 MINUTES

**MAKES:** EIGHT 4-INCH SANDWICHES OR FOUR 8-INCH SANDWICHES

### TOMATO CONFIT

10 Roma (plum) tomatoes, halved lengthwise

2 garlic cloves, minced

¼ cup extra-virgin olive oil

1 tablespoon fresh thyme

½ teaspoon red pepper flakes

¼ teaspoon kosher salt

¼ teaspoon freshly cracked black pepper

### CHICKPEA OLIVE TAPENADE

2 garlic cloves, peeled

1½ cups oil-cured black olives

2 tablespoons capers, drained

1 tablespoon fresh lemon juice

4 tablespoons olive oil

1½ cups canned chickpeas, drained and rinsed

¼ teaspoon freshly ground black pepper

### SANDWICHES

One 32-inch baguette

½ red onion, thinly sliced

4 jarred roasted red bell peppers

3 tablespoons balsamic reduction (see page 116)

12 fresh basil leaves, cut in half

Good olive oil

Salt and freshly cracked black pepper

**1 MAKE THE TOMATO CONFIT:** Preheat the oven to 300°F. Set a wire rack on top of a rimmed baking sheet.

**2** In a medium bowl, toss the tomatoes with the garlic, olive oil, thyme, and red pepper flakes until well coated. Arrange the tomato halves cut side up on the rack. Season with the salt and black pepper. Bake the tomatoes until shriveled and tender, 1 hour 30 minutes to 2 hours.

**3 MEANWHILE, MAKE THE TAPENADE:** In a food processor, pulse the garlic cloves to coarsely chop. Add the olives, capers, lemon juice, and 1 tablespoon of the olive oil and process into a smooth paste. Add 1 cup of the chickpeas and, with the motor running, drizzle in the remaining 3 tablespoons olive oil until the mixture is pureed. Transfer the puree to a small bowl and stir in the remaining ½ cup chickpeas, mashing them lightly with a fork. Season with the pepper.

**4 MAKE THE SANDWICHES:** Cut the baguette in half lengthwise. Spread the tapenade on the bottom half of the baguette, then add the onion and roasted peppers. Carefully spoon the tomato confit on top. Cut the basil leaves in half and place 9 halves on each sandwich. Drizzle the top half of the bread with olive oil and season with salt and freshly ground black pepper. Place the top of the baguette back on the sandwich. Wrap the sandwich tightly in plastic wrap. Leave in the refrigerator for at least 1 hour or up to overnight to develop the flavors.

# sausage sliders

I hate to play favorites, but these sliders are probably the most delicious things on our brunch menu. They're also the messiest, so if you're thinking of having royalty over for brunch, you might not want to serve these. Or at least, serve them with a whole lot of napkins. They're designed to be shared, as you'd be hard-pressed to fit anything else into your stomach after eating them. No reason to relegate them to breakfast menus, either, as they can be served at any meal.

**TIME:** 2 HOURS 30 MINUTES (INCLUDES TIME TO COOK SAUSAGE)

**MAKES:** 8 SLIDERS

**ROASTED FENNEL**

1 fennel bulb

1 tablespoon olive oil

½ teaspoon kosher salt

**CARAMELIZED ONIONS**

2 medium white onions

3 tablespoons olive oil

—

8 Pretzel Buns (page 97)

2 tablespoons Garlic Butter (page 17), melted

3 tablespoons Everything Spice (page 34)

¼ cup Romesco Aioli (page 38)

¼ cup Pickled Red Onions (page 42)

3 tablespoons olive oil

1 Italian Sausage (page 45), cut into ½-inch-thick rounds

1  Preheat the oven to 375°F.

2  **MAKE THE ROASTED FENNEL:** Halve the fennel bulb lengthwise and remove the outer layer, then slice the bulb lengthwise into ½-inch-thick pieces. Place the fennel on a rimmed baking sheet and toss with the olive oil and salt. Roast the fennel for 25 to 30 minutes, turning it once halfway through the cooking time. Remove from the oven and set aside to cool slightly.

3  **MAKE THE CARAMELIZED ONIONS:** Cut the onions in half through the root end, then thinly slice into half-moons. In a medium saucepan, heat the olive oil over medium-low heat. Add the onions and stir to coat with the oil. Cook for 15 to 20 minutes, stirring continuously, until a deep caramel color develops. Don't be tempted to turn the heat up, as this often leads to burning. Remove from the heat and set aside. Turn the oven to 350°F.

4  Split the buns in half crosswise and place them cut side up on a baking sheet. With a pastry brush, coat the top layer of each pretzel bun with the melted garlic butter. Sprinkle the everything spice liberally on top of each bun. Transfer the slider buns to a baking sheet. Spread the aioli on both sides of the slider buns. Divide the roasted fennel and the pickled red onions evenly among the

RECIPE CONTINUES ➔

bottom buns. Divide the caramelized onions evenly among the top buns. Place the slider buns in the oven to warm.

**5** In a medium saucepan, heat the olive oil over medium-high heat. Add the sausage and cook until crispy on both sides.

**6** Remove the slider buns from the oven. Divide the sausage pieces among the bottom buns, carefully cover with the top buns, and serve.

# pretzel buns

Why are pretzel buns so good? They remind me of teenage mall food, which is sort of sweetly nostalgic, but also of touring in Germany, where all sorts of pre-sobriety debauchery took place. Now I like to enjoy them with our Sausage Sliders (page 94) at brunch while sipping tea or maybe, if I'm really feeling wild, eat them with a latte.

**TIME:** 1 HOUR 30 MINUTES
**MAKES:** 12 SLIDER BUNS

¾ cup warm water

1 teaspoon active dry yeast

1 teaspoon sugar

2¼ cups bread flour

½ teaspoon kosher salt

½ cup plus 2 tablespoons Hard Butter (page 14), melted

½ teaspoon olive oil

2 tablespoons molasses

¼ cup baking soda

Everything Spice (page 34), for garnish

1  In the bowl of a stand mixer, stir together the water, yeast, and sugar. Set aside for 5 minutes, until the yeast is foamy.

2  Fit the stand mixer with the dough hook and add the flour, salt, and 2 tablespoons of the melted butter to the bowl. Begin mixing on low speed until the dough starts to come together, then increase the speed to medium-low and mix until the dough is smooth and comes away from the sides of the bowl.

3  Grease a large bowl with the olive oil. Transfer the dough to the oiled bowl, flipping the dough to coat it completely with the oil, and cover the bowl with a clean kitchen towel. Let stand in a warm area for about 1 hour, or until the dough has doubled in size.

4  Line a baking sheet with parchment paper. Punch down the dough and divide it into twelve equal pieces. Lightly knead each piece into a ball, tucking the sides underneath it and pinching them to seal. Roll each ball in your palm to smooth it out. Place the balls of dough on the prepared baking sheet. Cover with a clean kitchen towel and let rest for 30 minutes.

5  Preheat the oven to 425°F. Line a second baking sheet with parchment paper.

6  In a large pot, combine 8 cups of water and the molasses and bring to a boil over high heat. Slowly add the baking soda. Gently place four dough balls at a time into the water and boil for 30 seconds on each side. Remove from the water and place on the second parchment-lined baking sheet.

7  Using a very sharp knife or a lame, cut an "X" into the top of each ball of dough. Bake for 15 to 18 minutes, until the buns are very golden brown and sound hollow when you tap the bottom. Brush the tops of the buns with the remaining ½ cup melted butter and sprinkle with everything spice. Let cool completely before serving. Store in an airtight container for up to 1 week.

# little pine scramble

I have a strange prejudice against things that were on restaurant menus when I first became a vegan. To that end, I needed a lot of convincing to include a tofu scramble on our brunch menu, but I'm glad that we did, as it's delicious, filling, and a bit more virtuous than some of our other offerings. Wanna know the secret to its deceptively egg-like quality? Indian black salt, which adds the perfect sulfur component. You don't have to stick to our blueprint, either, as the scramble can be loaded with vegan cheese and just about any vegetables you like—within reason (our chef is English, and even *she* wouldn't use peas here).

**TIME:** 30 MINUTES

**SERVES:** 4 TO 6

### PICO DE GALLO

2 cups cherry tomatoes, quartered

¼ red onion, cut into small dice

2 teaspoons kosher salt

1 teaspoon olive oil

1 teaspoon fresh lemon juice

1 garlic clove, minced

1 tablespoon coarsely chopped fresh parsley leaves

### SCRAMBLE

2 pounds firm tofu

1½ tablespoons kala namak (black salt)

1 tablespoon onion powder

1 tablespoon granulated garlic

1 teaspoon ground turmeric

½ cup plus 2 tablespoons olive oil

¼ cup medium-diced red onion

¼ cup thinly sliced cremini mushrooms

¼ red bell pepper, cut into medium dice

¼ yellow bell pepper, cut into medium dice

¼ cup medium-diced Italian Sausage (page 45)

¼ cup store-bought tempeh bacon

3 cups spinach

**1 MAKE THE PICO DE GALLO:** In a medium bowl, combine the tomatoes, onion, salt, olive oil, lemon juice, garlic, and parsley. Set aside to let the flavors develop.

**2 MAKE THE SCRAMBLE:** Drain the tofu as much as possible. Crumble the tofu by hand, breaking it into small lumps into a medium bowl. Add the kala namak, onion powder, granulated garlic, turmeric, and ½ cup of the olive oil. Stir to combine and set aside.

**3** In a large skillet, heat the remaining 2 tablespoons olive oil over medium heat. Add the onion, mushrooms, and bell peppers. Cook, stirring frequently, 3 to 4 minutes or until soft. Add the sausage and bacon and cook for 2 to 3 minutes. Add the tofu mixture and cook, stirring frequently, until heated through. Remove from the heat and add the spinach. Stir until wilted. Serve piping-hot with a side of pico de gallo, and preferably with some freshly toasted buttered bread.

# frittata "egg" bake

Back before I became vegan, I never really liked eggs, which makes it even more surprising that I love this frittata. It's hearty, and perfect for mornings when you need something substantial and fueling rather than just filling. It's packed with protein and other nutrients, and powered by chickpea flour, nutritional yeast, and, of course, veggies. To that end, you can customize yours however you like; we serve it simply with potatoes, leeks, and onions, but any of your favorite vegetables will do.

**TIME:** 1 HOUR

**SERVES:** 4

1 cup chickpea flour

1 cup water

4 fingerling potatoes

4 ounces firm tofu, crumbled (about ½ cup)

3 tablespoons nutritional yeast

1¼ teaspoons kala namak (black salt)

1¼ teaspoons baking powder

¾ teaspoon ground turmeric

½ teaspoon kosher salt

½ teaspoon onion powder

¼ teaspoon freshly ground black pepper

¼ teaspoon chili powder

2 tablespoons olive oil

½ medium yellow onion, diced

1 medium leek, white part only, rinsed well and thinly sliced

1 tablespoon minced garlic

Nonstick cooking spray

¼ cup finely chopped fresh flat-leaf parsley, for serving

¼ cup finely chopped green onions, for serving

1  Preheat the oven to 350°F.

2  In a medium bowl, stir together the chickpea flour and water. Cover and refrigerate for at least 30 minutes or up to overnight.

3  Put the potatoes in a medium saucepan and add water to cover. Bring the water to a boil over medium-high heat and cook the potatoes until just tender. Drain and set aside to cool. When the potatoes are cool enough to handle, cut them into thin, even slices and set aside.

4  In a food processor, combine the chickpea mixture, tofu, nutritional yeast, kala namak, baking powder, turmeric, salt, onion powder, black pepper, and chili powder. Process until a smooth batter forms. Set aside.

5  In a medium saucepan, heat the olive oil over medium-low heat. Add the onion, leek, and garlic and sauté for about 10 minutes, until golden brown.

6  Coat an 8-inch ovenproof sauté pan with nonstick spray. Spread the onion mixture in an even layer over the pan. Arrange the sliced potatoes in a single layer on top of the onion mixture. Pour the chickpea batter over the vegetables and tilt the pan to distribute the batter as evenly as possible. Transfer the pan to the oven and bake for 35 minutes, or until golden brown. Remove from the oven and let cool for 10 minutes.

7  With a rubber spatula, free the edges of the frittata from the pan. Place a serving plate over the pan and invert the pan and plate together to release the frittata onto the plate. Top the frittata with the parsley and green onions before serving.

# soups
# and salads

# green gazpacho

The purist in me thinks gazpacho should be simple and traditional, but the sybarite in me thinks green gazpacho with an avocado base makes simple and traditional seem kind of dull. Besides, few things are more Californian than a bowl of liquid avocado. Serve this bright and uplifting soup as temperatures soar in the summer. It's refreshing but not insubstantial, thanks to the heartiness of everyone's favorite healthy fat–filled green fruit. This soup can be served by the bowlful or as an appetizer in small shooter servings.

**AHEAD:** STRAIN TOMATOES FOR 24 HOURS

**TIME:** 30 MINUTES (PLUS STRAINING TIME)

**SERVES:** 4

12 Roma (plum) tomatoes

½ cup olive oil

1 avocado, diced

1 cucumber, peeled, seeded, and chopped

1 bunch green onions, green parts only, chopped

2 garlic cloves, coarsely chopped

2 tablespoons fresh lemon juice

1 teaspoon kosher salt

Sliced radishes, for garnish (optional)

Microgreens, for garnish (optional)

1  In a high-speed blender, puree the tomatoes on high speed. Line a fine-mesh strainer with three layers of cheesecloth and set it over a large bowl or container. (Be careful to ensure that the strainer fits snugly in the bowl without falling over, and can comfortably fit in your fridge.) Carefully pour the tomato puree into the lined strainer. Place it in the fridge to strain overnight. After 8 hours, you will find about 1½ cups of clear tomato water in the bowl. If it's close, you can top it off with a little water. Discard the solids left in the strainer.

2  Transfer the tomato water to a high-speed blender and add the olive oil, avocado, cucumber, green onions, garlic, lemon juice, and salt. Blend on high speed until completely emulsified. Taste and adjust the seasoning if neeeded. Pour into serving bowls and garnish with radishes and microgreens, if desired.

# lemongrass and ginger butternut bisque

When things are calm at Little Pine, which thankfully isn't very often, we like to muse over interesting food combinations. This soup is the product of one of those conversations, although to be clear, it's delicious, not academic. It's also a year-round dish, as comforting in the cold of winter as it is light and breezy in the dead heat of (climate change-y) summer. P.S. Vegan diets reduce global warming—yay!

**TIME:** 1 HOUR 15 MINUTES

**SERVES:** 4

2 tablespoons canola oil

1 teaspoon kosher salt, plus more if needed

½ teaspoon ground coriander

½ teaspoon ground turmeric

2 cardamom pods

1 cinnamon stick

One 4-inch piece fresh lemongrass

1 tablespoon minced fresh ginger

1 small shallot, cut into small dice

1 small butternut squash, peeled, quartered, seeded, and cut into 2-inch pieces

4 sprigs cilantro

One 14-ounce can coconut milk

4 cups low-sodium vegetable broth, store-bought or homemade

1 teaspoon fresh lime juice

Unsweetened coconut yogurt, for serving (optional)

1 teaspoon black sesame seeds, for garnish

4 teaspoons chopped fresh mint or microherbs, for garnish (optional)

1  In a stockpot, heat the oil over medium heat. Add the salt, coriander, turmeric, cardamom pods, cinnamon stick, and lemongrass. Stir occasionally so as not to burn. Sauté the spices for 1 to 2 minutes, until fragrant. Add in the ginger and shallot and sauté for 5 to 6 minutes, stirring constantly, until the shallot starts to look translucent. Add the butternut squash and cilantro sprigs into the pot and then add the coconut milk and vegetable broth. Cover with a lid and bring to a boil over high heat. Once at a boil, reduce the heat to a simmer. Cook, covered, for an additional 30 to 45 minutes, or until the squash is soft and starting to fall apart. Remove the lemongrass, cardamom pods, and cinnamon stick and discard. Carefully transfer the soup to a high-speed blender with the lime juice and puree until smooth. Taste and season with more salt if needed.

2  Pour the soup into serving bowls. If desired, top each with 1 tablespoon of coconut yogurt, ¼ teaspoon of the sesame seeds, and 1 teaspoon of the mint, if desired.

# sunchoke soup

If you've never heard of a sunchoke, it's likely because they also go by the name of Jerusalem artichoke—even though they're from North America, which is nowhere near Israel, but I digress. Sunchokes are derived from a species of sunflower and are full of antioxidants, as well as tons of potassium and iron. Plus, they're earthy and delicious, sort of like a potato-artichoke hybrid. Thanks to these spud imposters and cashew cream, this minimalist soup is hearty and satisfying.

**TIME:** 1 HOUR

**SERVES:** 6

2 pounds sunchokes

2 tablespoons olive oil

1 small onion, sliced thinly

2 garlic cloves, minced

2 teaspoons kosher salt, plus more if needed

1 recipe Cashew Cream (page 18)

2 sprigs thyme

1 bay leaf

1 tablespoon white wine vinegar

1 Rinse the sunchokes in cold water, removing any dirt. Peel the sunchokes as best you can, then slice them as thinly as possible, placing them in a bowl of cold water as you go (this prevents them from oxidizing).

2 In a stockpot, heat the olive oil over medium heat. Add the onion and garlic and sauté until they are translucent. Drain the sunchokes and add them to the pot with the salt. Sauté for 5 to 7 minutes, until the sunchokes are tender and beginning to leach water. Add the cashew cream, thyme, and bay leaf to the pot. Reduce the heat to low, cover, and cook for 20 to 30 minutes, until the sunchokes are falling apart. Add the vinegar and turn off the heat. Remove the bay leaf and discard.

3 Carefully transfer the soup to a high-speed blender and puree until smooth and no lumps remain, 2 to 4 minutes, adding water ¼ cup at a time if needed to reach the desired consistency. Taste and adjust the seasoning if needed. Pour the soup into bowls and serve.

# mint pea soup

This simple soup embodies spring, as when peas come to the farmers' market, it's always the first sign that the season has sprung. My English chef tells me that pairing them with mint in this way is a very English combination, but to me, it makes sense here in LA, for both its seasonality and its airiness. If pea soup makes you think of some deep green sludge slumping out of a can, I encourage you to have your mind blown by how light and refreshing (and butter-free!) it can actually be. Serve it by the bowl or as shooters for a passed app or amuse-bouche.

**TIME:** 30 MINUTES

**SERVES:** 4

2 tablespoons Cultured Butter (page 16)

½ medium onion, cut into medium dice

2½ cups vegetable stock

3½ cups shelled fresh peas or thawed frozen peas

2 tablespoons fresh flat-leaf parsley leaves

2 tablespoons fresh mint leaves

1 teaspoon kosher salt, plus more if needed

½ teaspoon freshly ground black pepper, plus more if needed

1 tablespoon olive oil, for garnish

¼ cup plain unsweetened nondairy yogurt, for serving

1 tablespoon chopped fresh mint, for garnish

1  In a large heavy pot, melt the butter over medium heat. Add the onion and cook, stirring often, for 6 to 8 minutes, until softened but not browned. Add 1 cup of the stock and bring to a boil. Add the peas and reduce the heat to maintain a simmer. Cook until tender, about 5 minutes for fresh peas and 2 minutes for frozen. Remove the pot from the heat. Add the parsley, mint, salt, and the remaining 1½ cups stock to the pot. Carefully transfer the soup to a high-speed blender and puree until smooth, adding water ¼ cup at a time if needed to thin the soup. Add the pepper. Taste and adjust the seasoning if needed.

2  Pour the soup into serving bowls and top each with a drizzle of the olive oil, 1 tablespoon of the yogurt, and a scattering of the mint.

# potato leek soup

People love to say that Los Angeles doesn't have a winter, but on the three days a year when temperatures dip below 50 degrees, nothing is better than this hot, comforting soup. Though it's certainly not the fanciest dish in this book, to position this soup as simple is to do it a disservice. Also, the only thing better than hot soup on a cold day is hot soup with warm bread on a cold day, so I suggest serving this with slices of focaccia (page 142).

**TIME:** 45 MINUTES

**SERVES:** 6

6 sprigs thyme

1 bay leaf

2 tablespoons olive oil

3 large leeks, white and light green parts only, rinsed well and chopped

1 onion, cut into medium dice

1 garlic clove, chopped

5 cups water

1 medium potato, peeled and cut into medium dice

1 tablespoon Broth Powder (page 35)

1½ teaspoons kosher salt, plus more if needed

Pinch of freshly ground white pepper, plus more if needed

1 tablespoon chopped fresh chives, for garnish

**1**  Take a 4-inch square of cheesecloth and place the thyme and bay leaf in the center. Bring the corners together and tie an 8-inch length of kitchen twine around the bundle, leaving the ends of the twine free. Make sure the knot is secure so the contents can't fall out. Set the sachet of herbs aside.

**2**  In a medium saucepan, heat the olive oil over medium heat. Add the leeks, onion, and garlic and sauté until softened and beginning to caramelize. Add the water, potato, broth powder, sachet of herbs, salt, and white pepper. Simmer for about 30 minutes, until the potatoes are soft and cooked through.

**3**  Remove and discard the sachet of herbs. Carefully transfer the soup to a high-speed blender and blend on low speed until no lumps remain, adding water ¼ cup at a time if needed to reach the desired consistency. Taste and adjust the seasoning if needed. Pour into serving bowls and garnish with the chives.

# lentil soup

In 1990, I went to a little vegetarian restaurant in Montparnasse, France, that was run by a middle-aged husband and wife. The food was simple and provincial, yet their lentil soup was one of the best things I'd ever eaten. Lentil soup can be uninspiring, or it can be a simple combination of perfect, satisfying elements. I don't know that our soup is as good as the soup I had in Montparnasse, but it's certainly close.

**TIME:** 1 HOUR

**SERVES:** 4

1 sprig thyme

1 bay leaf

1 tablespoon neutral oil, such as canola oil

3 pieces store-bought tempeh bacon, cut into small dice

1 small onion, cut into small dice

1 garlic clove, minced

1½ tablespoons red wine

1 carrot, cut into small dice

1 celery stalk, cut into small dice

½ cup dried beluga lentils

3 cups water

1 small Dijon potato, peeled and cut into small dice

2 teaspoons Broth Powder (page 35)

1 teaspoon kosher salt, plus more to taste

½ teaspoon freshly ground black pepper, plus more if needed

**1** Take a 4-inch square of cheesecloth and place the thyme and bay leaf in the center. Bring the corners together and tie an 8-inch length of kitchen twine around the bundle, leaving the ends of the twine free. Make sure the knot is secure so the contents can't fall out. Set the sachet of herbs aside.

**2** In a stockpot, heat the oil over medium heat. Once hot, add the tempeh bacon and cook for about 2 minutes, until crispy. Add the onion and garlic and cook for 5 to 6 minutes, until the onion is translucent. Add the wine and stir, scraping up any browned bits from the bottom of the pan, and cook until the liquid has evaporated. Add the carrot and celery and cook for 4 to 5 minutes, until they start to soften. Add the lentils and stir to coat. Add the water, potato, sachet of herbs, broth powder, salt, and pepper. Bring to a boil, then reduce the heat to maintain a simmer. Cover and cook for about 30 minutes, until the lentils are tender. Remove and discard the sachet of herbs. Taste and adjust the seasoning if needed. Pour into serving bowls.

# watermelon caprese salad

This dish has become such a summertime staple for me that if I were to eat it in Patagonia in the dead of Southern Hemispheric winter, I'd have a Pavlovian reaction and still think I was in Los Angeles in July. Hopefully, it'll likewise transport you to your perfect summer idyll. The important thing to know about eating watermelon caprese is that you need to get the perfect balance of sweet and savory and umami in every bite. Oh, and the vegan mozzarella is one of the things on our menu that's most likely to elicit an incredulous "Are you sure this is vegan?" from dumbstruck customers. For this reason, you should serve this dish to friends who say they could never become vegan because of their love for cheese, and make converts of them all.

**TIME:** 45 MINUTES

**SERVES:** 4

½ cup balsamic vinegar

1 small seedless watermelon, washed and cut in half

1 pint cherry tomatoes, cut in half

12 balls Cashew Mozzarella (page 19), cut in half

18 fresh basil leaves

1 tablespoon flaky sea salt, such as Maldon, for finishing

1 In a small saucepan, bring the vinegar to a steady simmer over medium-high heat. Reduce the heat to low and simmer for about 7 minutes, until the vinegar has reduced by half. Remove the balsamic reduction from the heat.

2 Use a melon baller to scoop the watermelon into a medium bowl. Add the mozzarella to the bowl. Gently tear the basil leaves, add them to the mixture, and toss gently until all the ingredients are incorporated.

3 Spoon the mixture into serving bowls and generously drizzle with the balsamic reduction. Finish each salad with a dusting of flaky salt.

# heirloom red gem salad

Not to play aesthetic favorites, but this is probably our prettiest salad. It's fairly simple, but the gorgeous produce—Red Gem lettuce, watermelon radishes, and rainbow carrots—peacocks off the plate. There's substance behind its beauty, too; the subtly sweet Red Gems combine with slightly peppery radishes and tangy Dijon mustard dressing to create a dynamic and striking fresh flavor. Pro vegan tip: When shopping for Dijon mustard, be sure to find one that's actually vegan, as some commercially available Dijon mustards are not.

**TIME:** 30 MINUTES
**SERVES:** 4 TO 6

## MUSTARD DRESSING
*(makes about 1½ cups)*

1 teaspoon minced garlic

2 tablespoons minced shallot

¼ cup water

2 tablespoons champagne vinegar

2 tablespoons Dijon mustard

¼ teaspoon kosher salt

1 cup neutral oil, such as canola oil

## SALAD

4 heads Red Gem or red-leaf lettuce

1 small watermelon radish

3 rainbow carrots

1 tablespoon chopped fresh chives, for garnish

**1 MAKE THE MUSTARD DRESSING:** In a blender, combine the garlic, shallot, water, vinegar, mustard, and salt. Blend on high speed until completely smooth. With the blender running, slowly pour in the oil in a steady stream and blend to emulsify.

**2 MAKE THE SALAD:** Separate the lettuce leaves, wash them thoroughly, and pat dry. Place them in a large bowl and gently tear them.

**3** With a mandoline, carefully shave the radish into thin coins, then cut the coins into half-moons. Using the mandoline, shave the carrots from top to bottom to create long, thin ribbons. (If you don't have a mandoline, you can use a knife to cut the radish as thinly as you can and a vegetable peeler to shave the carrot into long, thin strips.) Add the carrots and radish to the bowl with the lettuce. Add the dressing to the salad, a few spoonfuls at a time, and toss until thoroughly coated. (You will have dressing left over; store it in an airtight container in the refrigerator for up to 1 week.)

**4** Taste and adjust the seasoning if needed. Transfer the salad to a serving bowl and garnish with the chives.

# caesar salad with chickpea croutons

We've taken a few liberties with our Caesar salad, and really, with its olives, tomatoes, chickpeas, and onions, it's more of a Caesar-Greek mash-up. I like to think of it as a "Caesar+"—plus nourishing veggies, and minus the little anchovies we prefer to let swim free.

**TIME:** 1 HOUR 35 MINUTES (PLUS 1 HOUR TO SOAK CASHEWS)

**SERVES:** 4

## CHICKPEA CROUTONS

One 15-ounce can chickpeas, drained and rinsed

1 teaspoon olive oil

1 teaspoon kosher salt, plus more if needed

½ teaspoon garlic powder

¼ teaspoon onion powder

## CAESAR DRESSING
*(makes 1 cup)*

1 cup raw cashews, soaked for 1 hour, then drained

½ cup water

2 teaspoons fresh lemon juice

2 teaspoons nutritional yeast

1 teaspoon kosher salt

1 teaspoon capers, drained

1 large garlic clove, minced

½ teaspoon Dijon mustard

½ teaspoon vegan Worcestershire sauce

1 tablespoon olive oil

## SALAD

10 ounces baby spinach

¼ cup thinly sliced red onion

1 cup halved cherry tomatoes

½ cup halved pitted kalamata olives

1 Preheat the oven to 400°F.

2 **MAKE THE CROUTONS:** Pat the chickpeas dry with a paper towel and place them on a rimmed baking sheet. Drizzle with the olive oil and toss to coat evenly. Season the chickpeas with the salt, garlic powder, and onion powder. Roast for 20 minutes. Remove from the oven and toss. Roast for 10 to 20 minutes longer, until crisp. Remove from the oven. Taste and adjust the salt if needed. Let cool completely.

3 **MAKE THE DRESSING:** In a high-speed blender, combine the cashews, water, lemon juice, nutritional yeast, salt, capers, garlic, mustard, and Worcestershire. Blend on high speed, stopping to scrape down the sides as necessary, until no lumps remain. With the blender running on low speed, slowly pour in the olive oil and blend to emulsify.

4 **MAKE THE SALAD:** Place the baby spinach in a large bowl. Add the dressing little by little until well coated. (You might have dressing left over; if so, store it in an airtight container in the refrigerator for up to 1 week.) Add the onion, tomatoes, and olives and mix well. Taste and adjust the seasoning if needed. Divide the salad among four serving bowls and top liberally with the chickpea croutons.

# seared radicchio salad

Salads aren't always describable as "robust," but this one certainly earns the moniker. It partners bitter grilled radicchio with sweet dates, toasted walnuts, smoky ricotta, herbs, and a balsamic dressing with sweet notes of agave to beautifully balanced effect. (P.S. If you've never grilled your salad greens, I suggest you start doing so ASAP.) The bitterness and smoky notes in this salad mean it's not for everyone, but for my friends who have adventurous palates, it's a favorite.

**TIME:** 30 MINUTES

**SERVES:** 4

**BALSAMIC DRESSING**

¼ cup balsamic vinegar

¼ cup mild agave nectar

1 tablespoon Dijon mustard

½ teaspoon kosher salt

½ cup olive oil

**SALAD**

3 heads radicchio

¼ cup plus 2 tablespoons olive oil

¼ cup walnuts

10 Medjool dates, halved lengthwise and pitted

¼ cup fresh tarragon leaves

¼ cup fresh parsley leaves

¾ cup Smoked Almond Ricotta (page 21)

1 teaspoon flaky sea salt, such as Maldon, for garnish

1  Preheat the oven to 350°F.

2  **MAKE THE DRESSING**: In a high-speed blender, combine the vinegar, agave, mustard, and salt. Blend on high speed, stopping to scrape down the sides as necessary, until no lumps remain. With the blender running on low speed, slowly pour in the olive oil and blend to emulsify.

3  **MAKE THE SALAD**: Peel away the outside layer of the radicchio leaves and quarter each head of radicchio lengthwise. Lay the radicchio quarters on a large baking sheet or platter and drizzle with ¼ cup of the olive oil.

4  In a large sauté pan, heat the remaining 2 tablespoons olive oil over medium-high heat. When the oil is hot, add the radicchio quarters, cut-side down, and cook until browned at the edges and firm-tender throughout, 3 to 5 minutes per side. Set the radicchio aside to cool.

5  Spread the walnuts evenly over a baking sheet. Toast in the oven for 5 to 10 minutes, being careful not to burn them. Thinly slice the dates lengthwise.

RECIPE CONTINUES →

**6** Core the radicchio quarters and cut them into bite-size pieces (around 1 inch). Transfer to a serving bowl and add the tarragon, parsley, walnuts, and dates. Toss gently to combine. Slowly pour the dressing onto the salad and toss until thoroughly dressed. Crumble the almond ricotta onto the top of the salad. Garnish with the flaky sea salt and serve.

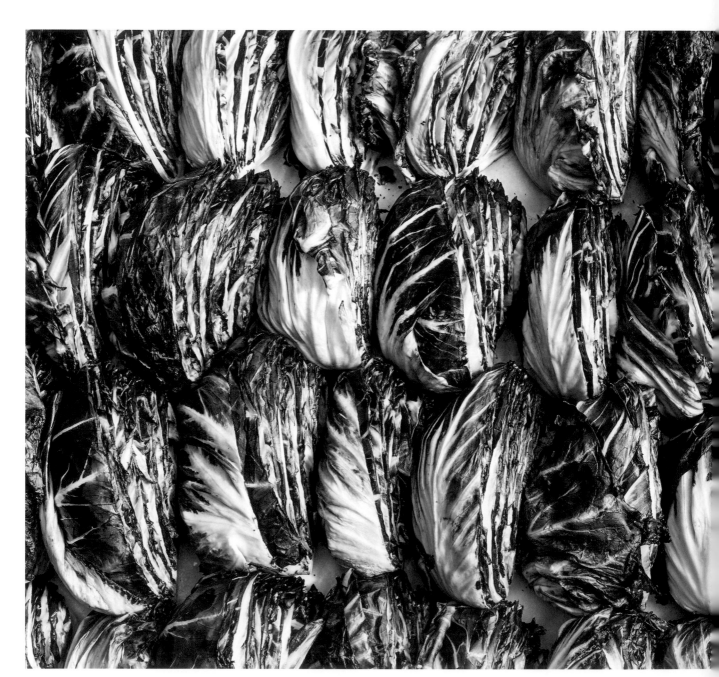

# panzanella salad

Much of what we serve at Little Pine is complex, as I spent my first few vegan decades eating the same basic foods over and over again. Now I love complicated, elaborate dishes, but I still love simple things, too, like this easy-to-make Tuscan salad. Composed in a traditional fashion, it modestly features just cherry tomatoes, cucumbers, basil, parsley and, of course, the homemade croutons that make a Panzanella a Panzanella.

**TIME:** 30 MINUTES

**SERVES:** 4 TO 6

**CROUTONS**

5 cups cubed crusty bread

3 tablespoons olive oil

1 teaspoon kosher salt

**VINAIGRETTE**
*(makes about 1½ cups)*

2 teaspoons minced garlic

2 tablespoons minced shallot

½ cup red wine vinegar

1 tablespoon Dijon mustard

1 teaspoon kosher salt

1 cup neutral oil, such as canola oil

**SALAD**

2 cups heirloom cherry tomatoes, cut in half

1 English (hothouse) cucumber, peeled, halved lengthwise, seeded, and cut into ¼-inch-thick slices

10 fresh basil leaves, thinly sliced

2 tablespoons coarsely chopped fresh parsley

Salt and freshly ground black pepper

1  Preheat the oven to 400°F.

2  **MAKE THE CROUTONS:** Toss the cubed bread with the olive oil and salt on a rimmed baking sheet. Toast in the oven for about 10 minutes, until lightly browned.

3  **MAKE THE VINAIGRETTE:** In a high-speed blender, combine the garlic, shallot, vinegar, mustard, and salt. Blend on high speed until completely smooth. With the blender running on low speed, slowly pour in the oil in a steady stream and blend to emulsify.

4  **MAKE THE SALAD:** In a large bowl, mix together the tomatoes, cucumber, basil, and parsley. Add the croutons and toss with enough vinaigrette to coat. (You will have vinaigrette left over; store it in an airtight container in the refrigerator for up to 1 week.) Season liberally with salt and pepper. Allow the salad to sit for 20 to 30 minutes before serving for the flavors to meld.

# walnut farro salad

At some point, salads got a bit of a bad name, but to me, this dish epitomizes what a true salad should be: a perfect medley of vegetables, nuts, and, in this case, fruits and grains, too. It's a winter salad, as evidenced by the inclusion of roasted butternut squash, seasonal pomegranate seeds, and warm cooked farro. The latter, by the way, is an excellent source of protein, as well as sleep-enabling magnesium and crucial B vitamins. I tend to spend my holidays in the studio making music and being reclusive, but if I were more social, I'd consider this a holiday potluck mainstay.

**TIME:** 45 MINUTES
**SERVES:** 4 TO 6

### SALAD

1 cup medium-diced peeled butternut squash

1 tablespoon olive oil

1 cup chopped walnuts

4 cups cooked farro

3 cups arugula

½ cup pomegranate seeds

### DRESSING

¼ cup white balsamic vinegar

1 tablespoon orange zest

2 tablespoons fresh orange juice

1 tablespoon agave nectar

1 teaspoon kosher salt, plus more if needed

½ cup olive oil

**1** Preheat the oven to 350°F. Line a baking sheet with parchment paper.

**2 MAKE THE SALAD:** Toss the squash in the olive oil and spread it on the prepared baking sheet. Roast for 15 to 20 minutes, until tender. Set aside.

**3** In a dry medium skillet, toast the walnuts over medium heat for 7 to 10 minutes, taking care to not let the nuts burn. Set aside.

**4** In a large bowl, combine the roasted squash, toasted walnuts, farro, arugula, and pomegranate seeds.

**5 MAKE THE DRESSING:** In a small bowl, whisk together the vinegar, orange zest, orange juice, agave, and salt. While whisking, slowly pour in the olive oil and continue whisking to emulsify.

**6** Slowly add the dressing to the salad and toss to coat. Taste and adjust the seasoning, if needed, then serve.

# small plates and sides

# roasted rainbow carrots with herb oil and smoked almond ricotta

For the longest time, paradoxically, vegan cooking seemed to avoid actual vegetables—maybe as a way of atoning for the culinary sins of hippies past. But it's been really inspiring to see vegan restaurants begin to do amazing things with produce, like this beta carotene–rich dish. I highly recommend you find a variety of different carrots for this recipe, as the dish really comes alive when you have the actual aforementioned rainbow carrots.

**TIME:** 45 MINUTES

**SERVES:** 4 TO 6

## HERB OIL

¼ cup fresh basil leaves

¼ cup fresh parsley leaves

1 cup olive oil

## ROASTED CARROTS

2 bunches rainbow carrots, with tops

¼ cup olive oil

¼ cup pure maple syrup

2 tablespoons fresh thyme leaves

1 teaspoon kosher salt

¼ teaspoon freshly ground black pepper

2 cups Smoked Almond Ricotta (page 21)

10 fresh basil leaves, thinly sliced, for garnish

**1** Preheat the oven to 350°F. Line a rimmed baking sheet with parchment paper.

**2** MAKE THE HERB OIL: In a high-speed blender, combine the basil, parsley, and olive oil. Blend on high speed, stopping to scrape down the sides as needed, until completely pureed. Pass through a fine-mesh strainer set over a bowl. Store the herb oil in an airtight container in the refrigerator for up to 3 days.

**3** MAKE THE ROASTED CARROTS: Rinse and scrub the carrots. Trim the carrot tops, leaving ¼ inch of the stem, and cut any overlarge carrots in half lengthwise. In a large bowl, toss the carrots with the olive oil, maple syrup, thyme, salt, and pepper. Place the carrots on the prepared baking sheet. Cover with aluminum foil and roast for 20 minutes, or until tender.

**4** Transfer the carrots to a serving tray and drizzle with ¾ cup of the herb oil. Using a spoon, take small pieces of the ricotta and place them on top of the carrots (store the remaining ricotta in an airtight container in the refrigerator for up to 1 week). Garnish with the basil and serve.

# grilled asparagus with chili-smoked almonds

Did you know that asparagus is also known as "sparrow grass"? Well, to be fair, neither did we, until we looked up asparagus online. This asparagus dish is surprisingly hearty, as the grilling adds a robust smoky quality to the otherwise dainty sparrow grass. We pair the charred greens with our in-house Chili-Smoked Almonds, which could go well with just about anything but seem especially well partnered in this dish.

**TIME:** 45 MINUTES
**SERVES:** 4

1 pound asparagus

2 tablespoons extra-virgin olive oil

1 teaspoon kosher salt

¼ cup Chili-Smoked Almonds (page 43)

1 teaspoon flaky sea salt

Heat a grill pan over high heat. Toss the asparagus with the olive oil and sprinkle with the salt. Place the asparagus spears on the grill pan. Grill the asparagus spears, turning them as needed to brown on all sides, for 2 to 4 minutes, until lightly charred and fork-tender. Transfer to a serving dish, sprinkle with the almonds and salt, and serve.

# garlic mashed potatoes

When my mom made mashed potatoes, she used an ungodly amount of butter and milk. Our recipe exemplifies the miracles of modern-day vegan cuisine, in that these taters taste just as decadent as Mom's, sans dairy.

**TIME:** 1 HOUR

**SERVES:** 4

3 pounds Idaho gold potatoes, peeled and halved

3 tablespoons kosher salt, plus more as needed

¼ cup Garlic Butter (page 17)

¼ cup Cashew Cream (page 18) or unsweetened unflavored nondairy milk

Freshly ground black pepper

Place the potatoes in a large pot and add water to just cover. Bring to a low boil over medium-high heat, add the salt, cover, and cook for 20 to 30 minutes, until the potatoes are soft. Drain thoroughly and transfer to a large bowl. Add the garlic butter and cashew cream. Use a potato masher or large fork to mash the potatoes until smooth. Season with salt and pepper and serve.

# crispy smashed potatoes with romesco aioli

I'm pretty sure these are the simplest things on our menu in terms of ingredients and preparation. I love to eat them, of course, but the inner child in me also just loves the idea of food that is, simply, smashed. (In a perfect world, I think you'd serve them with a mallet.) Plus, in my humble opinion, potatoes are underrated from a nutritional standpoint. Sure, they're not broccoli or kale, but potatoes are still packed with vitamin C, potassium, vitamin $B_6$, fiber, and antioxidants. Which is my way of saying—make these often, happily and guilt-free.

**TIME:** 1 HOUR

**SERVES:** 4

### VEGAN WORCESTERSHIRE POWDER

Nonstick cooking spray

2 tablespoons tomato powder

¼ cup kosher salt

¼ cup organic granulated sugar

1 tablespoon granulated garlic

1 tablespoon onion powder

½ teaspoon smoked paprika

¼ teaspoon lactic acid

### SMASHED POTATOES

1½ pounds fingerling potatoes

3 tablespoons olive oil

1 tablespoon chopped fresh chives, for garnish

1 cup Romesco Aioli (page 38), for serving

1  Preheat the oven to 450°F. Lightly oil a large baking sheet or coat it with nonstick spray.

2  **MAKE THE VEGAN WORCESTERSHIRE POWDER:** In a small bowl, combine the tomato powder, salt, sugar, granulated garlic, onion powder, paprika, and lactic acid. Set aside.

3  **MAKE THE SMASHED POTATOES:** Place the potatoes in a large pot and add water to cover. Bring to a boil and cook the potatoes until tender, 15 to 20 minutes, then drain well. Place the potatoes on the prepared baking sheet. Using a potato masher or fork, carefully smash the potatoes until flattened but still in one piece. Bake for 18 to 20 minutes, until golden brown and crisp. Transfer the potatoes to a medium bowl, sprinkle generously with the Worcestershire powder, and toss gently. Garnish with the chives and serve with the aioli.

# fried cauliflower with kimchi aioli

Adulthood is full of surprises—for example, realizing that I like cauliflower. When I was a little kid, even the word "cauliflower" seemed punitive. Now it's delicious, especially gently fried and served with kimchi aioli.

**TIME:** 45 MINUTES

**SERVES:** 4 TO 6 AS A SIDE

### KIMCHI AIOLI

½ cup vegan kimchi

1 tablespoon white miso paste

1 teaspoon paprika

1 teaspoon cayenne pepper

1 teaspoon minced fresh ginger

1 cup vegan mayonnaise

### FRIED CAULIFLOWER

Neutral oil, for frying

3 teaspoons kosher salt

2 heads cauliflower, cored and cut into bite-size florets

Leaves from 8 sprigs parsley, coarsely chopped

**1 MAKE THE KIMCHI AIOLI:** In a food processor, combine the kimchi, miso, paprika, cayenne, and ginger. Process into a paste.

**2** Transfer the kimchi paste to a small bowl and stir in the mayonnaise until thoroughly incorporated. Cover and refrigerate while you fry the cauliflower.

**3 MAKE THE FRIED CAULIFLOWER:** Fill a deep-fryer with neutral oil and heat the oil to 365°F. Line two baking sheets with paper towels.

**4** Fill a large pot (large enough to fit the cauliflower) with water three-quarters of the way. Add 2 teaspoons of the salt and bring to a boil over high heat. Drop the cauliflower into the pot and cook for 5 minutes until and fork-tender—be careful not to overcook. With a slotted spoon, remove the cauliflower from the water and place it on one of the paper towel–lined baking sheets to drain. Be careful to remove as much excess water as possible.

**5** Fry the cauliflower in the hot oil until golden brown, about 3 minutes per side, then use a slotted spoon to transfer it to the second paper towel–lined baking sheet to drain.

**6** Transfer the fried cauliflower to a serving bowl and toss with the remaining 1 teaspoon salt and the parsley. Serve with a side of kimchi aioli.

# broccoli arancini

Arancini means "little oranges" in Italian, which I suppose is what the inventors of the fried risotto balls known as arancini thought their creation resembled. To be clear, these broccoli arancini are savory, gently fried, in no way taste like citrus fruit, and would only look like one if you squinted in a dark room on a foggy day. With that settled, let's admit what makes this vegan version of the popular dish so special: the cheese sauce. (It's always the cheese sauce.)

**TIME:** 1 HOUR
**MAKES:** 24 ARANCINI

1 tablespoon olive oil

½ yellow onion, cut into small dice

3 garlic cloves, minced

3 cups uncooked Arborio rice

¼ cup white wine

1 tablespoon kosher salt

¾ cup Cheese Sauce (page 36)

2 cups broccoli florets, finely chopped

3 cups panko bread crumbs

⅓ cup canola oil or other neutral oil, for frying

¼ cup chopped fresh chives, for garnish

1 cup Pesto Aioli (page 38), for serving

**1** In a large sauté pan, heat the olive oil over medium heat. Add the onion and garlic and sauté for about 5 minutes, until translucent. Add the rice and stir to coat with the oil. Toast the rice for 3 to 4 minutes, being careful not to brown or burn it. Add the wine and stir, then cook until the alcohol has completely evaporated. Add ¾ cup water and the salt. Cook for 20 to 25 minutes, stirring occasionally, until the water has been absorbed. Continue to add water ½ cup at a time, allowing the rice to absorb the water after each addition, until the rice is completely cooked. Remove from the heat.

**2** Stir in the cheese sauce and the broccoli and let the mixture cool. Pack the mixture into a ¼-cup measuring cup to form a ball and turn it out onto a clean kitchen counter or work surface. Repeat with the remaining rice mixture; you will end up with about 24 balls. One by one, flatten each ball into a disc about 1 inch thick and 3 inches in diameter.

**3** Spread the panko over a shallow baking sheet. Dredge each disc of the rice mixture in the panko until completely coated.

**4** In a large pan, heat the canola oil over medium heat. Place six arancini in the pan and fry for 4 to 6 minutes, until golden brown on both sides. Repeat with the remaining arancini.

**5** Transfer the warm arancini to a platter. Garnish with the chives and serve with the aioli.

# focaccia

In the early days, bread was a vegan's best friend—especially on tours through towns where even veggies were hard to come by. These days I rely on it less for sustenance, but that has not at all impacted how often I indulge in it for pleasure. Few things add to the comfort level of a meal like warm, homemade bread, and this simple focaccia recipe is the culinary equivalent of a security blanket. Rich in olive oil, fragrant with rosemary, and surprising in its slight chile-flake bite, this fluffy bread pairs well with just about any savory supper.

**TIME:** 2 HOURS 15 MINUTES

**MAKES:** ONE 9 × 13-INCH LOAF

½ cup olive oil, plus more as needed

5⅓ cups unbleached all-purpose flour

1¾ cups warm water

2½ teaspoons kosher salt

1 teaspoon active dry yeast

5 teaspoons chopped fresh rosemary

¾ teaspoon red pepper flakes

2 teaspoons flaky sea salt, such as Maldon

**1**  Preheat the oven to 350°F. Brush a rimmed baking sheet with olive oil.

**2**  In the bowl of a stand mixer fitted with the dough hook, mix together the flour, warm water, salt, and yeast on low speed. With the mixer running, slowly stream in the olive oil and mix for 3 minutes, until all the ingredients are combined. Cover the bowl with a clean kitchen towel and set aside in a warm place for 1 hour, or until the dough has doubled in size.

**3**  Transfer the dough to the prepared baking sheet. Brush the dough with olive oil and cover with a clean kitchen towel. Set aside for 20 minutes, until the dough has puffed up and risen a bit more.

**4**  With your fingertips, gently press down on the surface of the dough, extending it out to all edges of the baking sheet and creating small indents. Drizzle more olive oil over the dough and sprinkle it with the rosemary, red pepper flakes, and flaky salt.

**5**  Bake for 25 to 30 minutes, until golden brown. Let cool completely before slicing. Store, covered, at room temperature for up to 2 days.

# charred broccolini with chili-smoked almonds, pickled onions, and chipotle aioli

Broccolini is a sweeter, milder broccoli hybrid that—fun fact—has only been around since the early '90s, when I was more or less squatting in an abandoned factory in New York City and subsisting on oats and raisins. You can simply sauté, steam, or roast this nutrient-dense food, but for the restaurant we've created a slightly more elevated take. Our approach pairs the green with smoky almonds, pickled onions, and chipotle aioli to create the perfect side to any protein-centric or pasta main. I guess the fact that I eat this regularly makes me wonder why so many people still think veggies are dull.

**TIME:** 1 HOUR

**SERVES:** 4 TO 6

**CHIPOTLE AIOLI**

4 garlic cloves, peeled

1 teaspoon olive oil

One 7-ounce can chipotle chiles in adobo sauce, sauce drained off

1 cup vegan mayonnaise

**CHARRED BROCCOLINI**

2 bunches Broccolini

2 tablespoons olive oil

Juice of ½ lemon

Kosher salt

Nonstick cooking spray

1 cup Chili-Smoked Almonds (page 43), for serving

1 cup Pickled Red Onions (page 42), for serving

1  Preheat the oven to 350°F.

2  **MAKE THE CHIPOTLE AIOLI:** In a small bowl, toss the garlic with the olive oil. Place on a small baking sheet and roast for 8 to 10 minutes. Remove from the oven and let cool, then transfer the roasted garlic to a small food processor, add the chipotle chiles, and process into a paste. Carefully transfer the paste to a small bowl. Add the mayonnaise and mix thoroughly. Cover and refrigerate while you cook the Broccolini.

3  **MAKE THE CHARRED BROCCOLINI:** Heat a grill pan over medium-high heat.

RECIPE CONTINUES ➔

**4** Place the Broccolini in a medium bowl and drizzle with the olive oil and lemon juice. Season with salt and toss to coat. Spray the grill pan with cooking spray, then add the Broccolini and grill for 6 to 8 minutes until charred, turning once.

**5** Transfer the Broccolini to a serving dish, sprinkle the almonds on top, and finish with the pickled red onions. Serve family-style, with the aioli alongside.

# moby's kitchen

When I'm at Little Pine, I eat like a sybarite (which, by the way, is a great word—the only downside to using it in a sentence is that most people will have no idea what it means), but when I'm home, I eat fairly monastically.

My solo diet is relatively unchanged from how I ate when I became a vegan thirty years ago: brown rice, beans, nuts, and broccoli. I like eating this way, but I make a point of not cooking this way for friends (or at Little Pine), as I'm generally interested in keeping the few friends I have.

Although these recipes are a bit more decadent than brown rice and steamed broccoli, here are the two I default to most often.

CONTINUES →

# moby's daily smoothie

One of the slightly more indulgent staples of my monastic diet is my daily smoothie. It's sweet, but also incredibly healthy and good for you.

The other recipes in the book are quite specific, but the recipe for my daily smoothie is as vague as an E. E. Cummings poem or a Thurston Moore guitar solo.

It's largely up to you what you choose to include, so feel free to experiment as much or as little as you want.

——

We'll start with the base:

- 1 **banana**, frozen

- 1½ cups **liquid** (I use water, but you can use any type of vegan milk if you want a creamier smoothie)

- Some **ice** (Or not. Again, dealer's choice. And you can of course add more water if your smoothie is too thick.)

——

And now the electives . . . and forgive me for not being more specific, but what you include really is up to you. I do recommend trying a few from each category in each smoothie, for taste and nutrition.

- **Fruits** (use generously): Blackberries, blueberries, raspberries, strawberries, peaches, red or black grapes, cranberries, pineapple

- **Vegetables** (use generously): Red chard, kale, spinach, red cabbage, carrots, broccoli, broccoli sprouts

- **Fiber** (maybe 1 teaspoon or less—to be honest, you can refrain from adding extra fiber, as everything in the smoothie is already loaded with fiber. But fiber is really one of the ultimate superfoods . . . and without fiber your healthy gut bacteria have nothing to eat): Flaxseeds, chia seeds, psyllium husks, inulin

- **Adaptogens and fun extras** (use sparingly): Fresh ginger, fresh or ground turmeric, powdered mushrooms, raw cacao nibs or unsweetened cacao powder, vegan DHA oil

And there you have it! Be creative, have fun, and figure out what you love. And then once you've figured out what you love, try swapping out one thing for another and adding things you haven't tried. If you want to include something I haven't listed here, then by all means, do—add cashews, avocado, spirulina, it's really up to you.

Also, you'll notice that everything listed here is almost absurdly healthy . . . and the right combination gives you a smoothie that's fantastically high in fiber, phytonutrients, and healthy oils.

Another note: The abundance of fiber and antioxidants in a good daily smoothie means that the relative sweetness shouldn't cause insulin spikes or read very high on the glycemic index.

# kimchi pasta e fagioli

This is my go-to for a quick, interesting, tasty, and exceedingly healthy meal at home.

   If you use good kimchi, this meal covers all the bases: fiber, protein, fermented food, omega-3s, and tons of antioxidants. Plus, it's really easy to make.

**TIME:** 10 MINUTES • **SERVES:** 1

½ cup dried conchiglie (shells) pasta

¼ cup vegan kimchi, plus more as desired

½ cup canned black beans, drained and rinsed

1 tcaspoon raw walnuts

1 teaspoon sprouted hulled pumpkin seeds

1 tablespoon olive oil

Pinch of sea salt

Pinch of cayenne pepper

Bring a medium pot of water to a boil. Cook the pasta to your desired doneness. Drain, but don't rinse, the pasta, then transfer it to a bowl. Add the kimchi to taste (use a lot, if possible), the black beans, walnuts, pumpkin seeds, and olive oil. Mix everything together. Season with the salt and cayenne and enjoy.

# farinata with mozzarella and romesco sauce

Technically a chickpea flour pancake, I think of farinata as more of a nutrient-dense mini pizza crust. In other words, it's a wonderful vehicle for delivering all sorts of deliciousness. In the restaurant, we top it with our housemade mozzarella and romesco sauce, as well as arugula and olives, but you can smother it with just about any of your favorite veggies and sauces. Somehow simultaneously light yet substantial, it's best when shared as an appetizer or even prepared as a single-serve savory breakfast or lunch. Eat while fresh and hot.

**TIME:** 1 HOUR

**SERVES:** 6

2 cups chickpea flour

2 cups water

¼ cup olive oil, plus more for cooking

1 tablespoon minced fresh rosemary

1 teaspoon kosher salt

1 teaspoon freshly ground black pepper

**TOPPINGS**

1 cup Romesco Sauce (page 37)

½ cup coarsely chopped pitted kalamata olives

6 balls Cashew Mozzarella (page 19)

3 cups baby arugula

Good olive oil

Flaky sea salt, such as Maldon

**1**  Preheat the oven to 350°F.

**2**  In a medium bowl, whisk together the chickpea flour, water, olive oil, rosemary, salt, and pepper until combined and no lumps remain. The mixture should resemble pancake batter. Let the batter rest at room temperature for 30 minutes.

**3**  In a 5-inch nonstick frying pan, heat 2 tablespoons of the olive oil over medium heat, swirling the pan to coat. Pour ½ cup of the batter into the pan and swirl the pan to coat the bottom in an even layer of batter. Cook until the edges start to brown, 3 to 4 minutes, then flip the farinata and cook for another 3 to 4 minutes, until brown and crispy on the second side, then slide it onto a plate. Repeat with the remaining oil and batter.

**4**  Lay the farinatas out in a single layer on baking sheets. Spread the romesco sauce in an even layer over the top. Evenly distribute the olives and mozzarella among the farinatas. Transfer the pan to the oven and bake for 10 to 12 minutes to warm through. Remove from the oven and garnish each farinata with ½ cup of the arugula. Drizzle with good olive oil and sprinkle with flaky salt, then serve.

# roasted kalettes with fresno chile

Oh, science—one day putting people on the moon, the next day inventing kale–Brussels sprout hybrids. Kalettes are a farmers' market favorite, at least here in Southern California. We bake them until they're crispy with a hint of caramelization and then top them with Fresno chiles. The result is a dish that's fresh and simple yet spicy—plus, it is science and the future.

**TIME:** 30 MINUTES
**SERVES:** 4

1 pound Kalettes

2½ tablespoons olive oil

2 teaspoons red wine vinegar

¼ teaspoon sea salt

1 small Fresno chile, thinly sliced

1  Preheat the oven to 450°F.

2  Trim the ends from the Kalettes. Place them in a medium bowl. Add the olive oil, vinegar, and salt and toss well. Spread the Kalettes evenly over a baking sheet. Roast for about 12 minutes, until they are cooked through and crisp on the outside, flipping them midway through the cooking time. Remove from the oven. Garnish with the chile and serve piping hot.

# maitake crostini

I love serving this to my friends who claim to not like mushrooms, as after eating the maitake crostini, they end up becoming people who actually like mushrooms. Once the buttery bread is slathered with pesto and topped with piles of mushrooms, it becomes irresistible, the perfect passed appetizer for your next dinner party. Plus, mushrooms are medicine—the delicious kind only Mother Nature makes.

**TIME:** 45 MINUTES
**MAKES:** 14 CROSTINI

### CROSTINI

¼ day-old baguette, cut on an angle into fourteen ¼-inch-thick slices

¼ cup olive oil

1 teaspoon granulated garlic

¼ teaspoon sea salt

### HERB-ROASTED MAITAKES

One 8-ounce container maitake (hen-of-the-woods) mushrooms

3 tablespoons extra-virgin olive oil

1 teaspoon finely chopped fresh rosemary

1 teaspoon finely chopped fresh thyme

Pinch of sea salt

—

1½ cups Pesto Aioli (page 38), for serving

10 leaves fresh basil, thinly sliced, for garnish

**1** Preheat the oven to 350°F. Line a baking sheet with parchment paper.

**2 MAKE THE CROSTINI:** Brush both sides of each slice of bread with the oil and sprinkle both sides with the granulated garlic and salt. Place the bread on the prepared baking sheet and bake for about 7 minutes, until golden brown. Remove from the oven and set aside. Raise the oven temperature to 400°F.

**3 MAKE THE HERB-ROASTED MAITAKES:** Line a large baking sheet with parchment paper. Break the mushrooms into small clusters and place them in a medium bowl. Drizzle with the olive oil and add the rosemary, thyme, and salt. Toss to coat. Spread the mushrooms evenly over the prepared baking sheet and roast for about 15 minutes, until golden brown and slightly crispy on the edges.

**4** Spread the aioli over one side of each crostini and arrange them on a serving platter. Top evenly with the mushrooms and garnish with the basil.

# salt-cured beets with arugula, almond ricotta, and balsamic dressing

Confession: I don't like cooked beets. Yes, I know . . . I'm weird. I'm assured by those who are fans of the root veggie, however, that this dish is quite delicious, and I'm inclined to believe them, given that it's hard to go wrong with sugar, salt, and cheese (in this case, our housemade ricotta). Arugula adds a little spiciness to the flavor profile of this shared plate, and balsamic dressing ties the medley together.

**TIME:** 2 HOURS
**SERVES:** 6

One 3-pound box kosher salt

4 medium beets

5 sprigs fresh thyme

2 cups arugula

1 cup Almond Ricotta (page 20)

½ cup Balsamic Dressing (see page 123)

Pinch of flaky sea salt, such as Maldon

1 tablespoon slivered almonds, for garnish

**1** Preheat the oven to 350°F.

**2** In a high-sided baking dish, sprinkle a thin layer of the salt. Add the beets, making sure they do not touch. Place the thyme on top of the beets. Cover the beets with the remaining salt and bake for about 1 hour 15 minutes, until fork-tender. Remove from the salt. Peel the beets; the skins should slip right off. Slice the beets into thin rounds using a mandoline or sharp knife.

**3** Arrange the beets on a plate of your choice. Scatter the arugula and almond ricotta over the beets. Drizzle with the dressing and finish with flaky salt and the slivered almonds.

# sriracha-glazed seared brussels sprouts

Growing up, I, like many people, loathed and feared Brussels sprouts. Now, because of this dish, I've turned into someone who actually craves them. What makes these simple vegan gems so remarkable and addictive is the combination of pan-searing then roasting them before coating them in a spicy-sweet sriracha glaze; the result is almost like a veggie candy. I hope this recipe—one of Little Pine's most popular—can likewise help you trade your childhood sprout aversion for a cruciferous vegetable obsession.

**TIME:** 30 MINUTES

**SERVES:** 4 AS A SIDE

### SRIRACHA GLAZE

¼ cup sriracha

¼ cup agave nectar

¼ cup sesame oil

2 tablespoons tamari

1 tablespoon fresh lime juice

### BRUSSELS SPROUTS

2 tablespoons vegetable oil

1 pound Brussels sprouts, trimmed and halved

1 teaspoon white sesame seeds, for garnish

1  Preheat the oven to 350°F.

2  **MAKE THE SRIRACHA GLAZE:** In a small bowl, whisk together the sriracha, agave, sesame oil, tamari, and lime juice until incorporated. Set aside.

3  **MAKE THE BRUSSELS SPROUTS:** In a medium cast-iron skillet large enough to fit all the Brussels sprouts, heat the vegetable oil over medium-high heat until almost smoking. (If you don't have a pan large enough, cook the Brussels sprouts in two pans; divide the oil evenly between them.) When the oil is hot, place the Brussels sprouts cut side down in the pan, reduce the heat to medium, and cook for about 3 minutes, until dark brown. Stir thoroughly and cook for 2 minutes more. Transfer the skillet to the oven and bake for 10 minutes. Remove the skillet from the oven and toss the Brussels sprouts with enough glaze to coat them evenly. (If you have any glaze left over, store it in an airtight container in the refrigerator for up to 1 week.) Garnish the Brussels sprouts with the sesame seeds and serve.

# hearty mains and large plates

# autumn risotto

Rice is a dear old friend of any vegan, but, having grown up poor in the suburbs, it was fairly late in life that I took my first bite of risotto, its fanciest iteration. It was worth the wait, and later, it was a no-brainer to add risotto to our Little Pine menu. What's most surprising about this particular recipe—to me as a humble restaurant owner rather than a chef, at least—is its relative simplicity; it tastes like it's difficult to make, but it's not. In fact, it's one of those recipes for which you're bound to have most of the ingredients already in your pantry, with a run to the farmers' market needed only for onions, maitake mushrooms, garlic, herbs, and this dish's costar: butternut squash (top billing goes to the rice, of course). As its name implies, this is the perfect dish for a perfect fall day—clear, crisp, and colorful.

**TIME:** 1 HOUR
**SERVES:** 4

One 8-ounce package maitake (hen-of-the-woods) mushrooms

3 tablespoons olive oil

Salt and freshly ground black pepper

5 cups vegetable stock

2 tablespoons olive oil

1 medium onion, cut into small dice

1 garlic clove, minced

2 cups uncooked Arborio rice

¼ cup white wine

2½ cups medium-diced peeled butternut squash

1 cup Cashew Cream (page 18)

1 tablespoon minced fresh rosemary

1  Preheat the oven to 425°F.

2  With a knife, remove the woody stem from the maitake cluster. Break the maitakes into equal pieces. Toss the maitakes in a bowl with 1 tablespoon of the olive oil and season with salt and pepper. Spread them evenly over a baking sheet and roast for 10 minutes. Remove the maitakes from the oven and toss, then roast for 10 minutes more. Check for doneness; the maitakes should be golden brown and slightly crispy on the edges. Remove from the oven and let cool to room temperature.

3  In a small saucepan, bring the stock to a simmer over medium-low heat. In a large saucepan, heat the remaining 2 tablespoons olive oil over medium heat. Add the onion and garlic. Cook for about 5 minutes, stirring often, until soft and translucent. Add the rice and stir continuously for 1 minute to toast the grains. Add the wine and stir until it has been completely absorbed. Add ½ cup of the hot stock and cook, stirring continuously, until liquid has been almost completely absorbed. Add another ½ cup of the stock and cook, stirring continuously, until liquid has been almost completely absorbed. Stir in the squash and continue adding the stock ½ cup at a time, making sure that most of the liquid has been absorbed before adding more, until the rice is firm but tender. This will take about 25 minutes; start checking the doneness of the rice when you have about 1 cup of stock left. Stir in the cashew cream and rosemary. Taste and adjust the seasoning if needed. Garnish each serving with the roasted maitakes and serve.

# celery root cassoulet

Cassoulet is a stewlike French dish named after the vessel in which it's cooked, and it's deceptively complex for a comfort food. While the cooking process is involved, that intricacy results in a massive, savory payoff. One of its key ingredients is a star food that doesn't get the attention it deserves: celery root. Our chef loves this homely vegetable for its versatility and robust flavor profile. While it can be roasted as a main, pureed as a soup or mashed potato substitute, or sliced and served as a garnish, here it's simply diced. Serve this cassoulet on a cold day, before or after playing in the snow.

**AHEAD:** SOAK THE CANNELLINI BEANS OVERNIGHT

**TIME:** 1 HOUR 30 MINUTES (PLUS SOAKING OVERNIGHT)

**SERVES:** 8

## VEGETABLE MIREPOIX

2 cups medium-diced carrots

2 cups medium-diced peeled celery root

1 cup medium-diced onion

2 tablespoons olive oil

1 teaspoon kosher salt

¼ teaspoon freshly ground black pepper

## CANNELLINI BEANS

8 ounces dried cannellini beans, soaked overnight, then drained

1 large onion, cut in half

2 carrots, cut into large pieces

1 head garlic, halved crosswise

4 sprigs thyme

1 bay leaf

1 teaspoon freshly ground black pepper

Kosher salt

## SAUCE

1 tablespoon olive oil

½ yellow onion, cut into medium dice

1 shallot, minced

2 garlic cloves, crushed and peeled

⅓ cup red wine

Two 16-ounce cans crushed tomatoes

1 cup vegetable stock

4 sprigs parsley

3 sprigs thyme

3 fresh basil leaves

1 bay leaf

¼ teaspoon fennel seeds

1 star anise pod

1 recipe Herbed Bread Crumbs (page 47), for topping

1  Preheat the oven to 350°F. Line a baking sheet with parchment paper.

2  **MAKE THE VEGETABLE MIREPOIX:** In a medium bowl, toss together all ingredients. Transfer to the prepared baking sheet and bake for 20 to 25 minutes, until cooked thoroughly. Set aside.

3  **MAKE THE CANNELLINI BEANS:** In a large pot, combine the beans, onion, carrots, garlic, thyme, bay leaf, and pepper. Add water to the pot until all the ingredients are covered by 2 inches. Cover the pot with the lid ajar and bring the water to a boil. Cook the beans, skimming the surface occasionally and adding more water as needed to keep the beans submerged, for about 30 minutes, then season with salt and cook for 15 minutes more, or until the beans are tender but not falling apart. Remove the pot from the heat and carefully drain the beans in a strainer set over a metal bowl. Discard the onion, carrots, garlic, thyme, and bay leaf.

4  **MAKE THE SAUCE:** In a medium pot, heat the olive oil over medium heat. Add the onion, shallot, and garlic and sauté for 5 to 7 minutes, until translucent. Add the wine, tomatoes, and stock. Bring to a simmer. Add the parsley, thyme, and basil to the pot. Take a 4-inch square of cheesecloth and place the fennel seeds and star anise in the center. Bring the corners together and tie an 8-inch length of kitchen twine around the bundle, leaving the ends of the twine free. Add the sachet to the sauce. Simmer over medium heat for 30 minutes. Remove the sachet.

5  Stir the mirepoix and cannellini beans into the sauce. Taste and adjust the seasoning if needed. Carefully transfer the mixture to a casserole dish approximately 10 × 8 inches and top with the bread crumbs. Bake for 20 to 30 minutes, until the bread crumbs are golden.

# fennel flatbread pizza

In 2017, we had a staff Christmas party, and my genius colleagues at Little Pine made this pizza for themselves. I had a piece, loved it, and was baffled—why hadn't we been serving this in the restaurant? Not surprisingly, it's been on the menu forever after December 26, 2017. The key is our housemade vegan sausage. And the amazing pizza dough. And the fennel. Okay, there are a lot of keys that together make this another one of those dishes that is a bit earth-shaking for nonvegans, as it changes their perception of what plant-based food can be.

**TIME:** 1 HOUR

**MAKES:** 2 FLATBREADS

## DOUGH

⅔ cup lukewarm water

½ teaspoon agave nectar

1½ teaspoons active dry yeast

2 cups unbleached all-purpose flour plus more for dusting.

½ teaspoon kosher salt

## TOPPINGS

1 bulb fennel, trimmed and cleaned

2 tablespoons olive oil

½ teaspoon kosher salt

1 cup packed spinach

2½ cups Romesco Aioli (page 38)

1 teaspoon fennel seeds

1 cup small-diced Italian Sausage (page 45)

1 cup vegan shredded parmesan

2 teaspoons crushed red pepper flakes

**1  MAKE THE DOUGH:** In the bowl of a stand mixer, stir together the water, agave, yeast, and salt. Let stand for 5 to 10 minutes, depending on how warm your kitchen is, until the yeast blooms and the mixture becomes bubbly. Add the flour and, using the dough hook, mix on medium speed until completely combined. The dough will be sticky to the touch. Portion the dough into two equal 6-ounce portions. In two small well-oiled bowls, add one dough portion to each bowl. Allow to proof for about 20 minutes or until doubled in size.

**2  MAKE THE TOPPINGS:** While the dough proofs, preheat the oven to 425°F. To trim the fennel bulb, halve it lengthwise and remove the outer layer. Slice the remaining pieces lengthwise into ½-inch-thick pieces. On a rimmed baking sheet, coat the fennel with 1 tablespoon of the olive oil and the salt. Roast for 25 to 30 minutes, turning over once halfway through the cooking time. Set aside to cool slightly.

**3**  Reduce the oven temperature to 350°F.

**4**  Heat the remaining 1 tablespoon olive oil in a small saucepan over medium heat. Add the spinach and sauté for 2 to 3 minutes, until wilted. Set aside.

**5**  Roll one portion of dough on a floured surface into approximately a 10 × 4-inch oval. The dough should be extremely thin at this point.

**6**  Place the flatbread on a well-floured parchment-covered flat baking sheet.

**7**  Divide the romesco aioli between the two pizza crusts and spread with the back of a spoon. Cover each crust with the roasted fennel and spinach. Sprinkle with the fennel seeds and evenly distribute the sausage. Lastly, top with the vegan parmesan.

**8**  Bake the flatbreads for 20 to 30 minutes until the pizza is cooked through and crisp on the outside. Remove the flatbreads from the oven and serve!

# fettuccine alfredo with shiitake crisp

Traditional fettuccine Alfredo is made with loads of butter and cheese, so it's not a glaringly obvious choice for vegan conversion. Fortunately, cashew cream, olive oil, and vegan parmesan substitute here to create plant-based decadence, and crumbled shiitake crisp then finishes off the over-the-top savory taste of this comforting classic. It's a dish I recommend serving to nonvegans who aren't yet ready for something more veggie-centric, or for whipping up when you're simply craving *formaggio*.

**AHEAD:** SOAK CASHEWS FOR 2 HOURS OR UP TO OVERNIGHT

**TIME:** 1 HOUR (PLUS SOAKING TIME)

**SERVES:** 6

### CREAM SAUCE

2 teaspoons olive oil

½ large yellow onion, cut into small dice

5 garlic cloves, minced

2 cups raw cashews, soaked for at least 2 hours or up to overnight, then drained

¼ cup pine nuts, toasted

1 tablespoon white miso paste

1 teaspoon Dijon mustard

1 cup Cashew Cream (page 18)

¾ cup water

2 teaspoons kosher salt

Pinch of lemon zest

### PASTA

1 pound dried fettuccine

3 tablespoons olive oil

¼ cup white wine

½ cup fresh or frozen peas

Pinch of flaky sea salt, such as Maldon, plus more if needed

¼ teaspoon cracked black pepper, plus more if needed

1 cup Shiitake Crisp (page 41)

½ cup fresh flat-leaf parsley, coarsely chopped, for garnish

½ cup grated vegan parmesan, for garnish

1 **MAKE THE CREAM SAUCE:** In a small sauté pan, heat the olive oil over medium-high heat. Add the onion and garlic and sauté until translucent. Transfer the onion mixture to a high-speed blender and add the cashews, pine nuts, miso, mustard, cashew cream, water, salt, and lemon zest. Start the blender on low speed and wait for the ingredients to start getting incorporated, then slowly turn the blender up to high speed and blend until the mixture is silky-smooth with no visible lumps.

2 **MAKE THE PASTA:** Bring a large pot of water to a boil. Cook the fettuccine according to the package instructions until al dente. Drain the pasta, transfer it to a bowl, and toss with the olive oil. Set aside.

3 Heat a large saucepan over high heat. Add the wine and quickly add the cream sauce, peas, salt, pepper, ½ cup of the shiitake crisp, and the cooked pasta. Stir until warmed throughout. Taste and adjust the seasoning if needed. Do not overheat, as the sauce might seize. Transfer to a plate and garnish with pepper, the remaining ½ cup shiitake crisp, the parsley, and parmesan.

# mac and cheese

It was a big day in the land of vegan when we all realized you could make this nostalgic pasta dish without dairy, and that the healthier, cruelty-free version could actually be great. We must have done something right with ours, because it's a favorite among the nonvegans who frequent the restaurant, a tough crowd to convert when it comes to anything cheese-related. Sometimes, tables order it twice in one sitting—is there any better compliment?

**TIME:** 45 MINUTES
**SERVES:** 4

12 ounces dried elbow macaroni

2 tablespoons extra-virgin olive oil

4 slices white bread, stale or lightly toasted

½ teaspoon kosher salt

1 recipe Cheese Sauce (page 36)

½ cup shredded vegan parmesan

1 tablespoon chopped fresh chives, for garnish

**1** Preheat the oven to 350°F.

**2** Bring a large ovenproof saucepan of water to a boil. Cook the macaroni according to package instructions. Drain completely and cool under cold running water. Return the noodles to the saucepan and drizzle with 1 tablespoon of the olive oil; toss well so the noodles do not stick together.

**3** Meanwhile, tear the bread into small pieces, put them in a food processor, and process into coarse crumbs. Spread the bread crumbs in an even layer over a large rimmed baking sheet. Toast in the oven for 8 to 10 minutes, stirring occasionally, until browned and dry. Remove from the oven; turn on the broiler.

**4** Transfer the hot bread crumbs to a large bowl. Drizzle with the remaining 1 tablespoon olive oil, add the salt, and toss. Let cool completely. (If you won't be using them immediately, store the bread crumbs in an airtight container at room temperature for up to 1 month.)

**5** Pour the cheese sauce onto the pasta and heat over medium heat until piping-hot. Add ¼ cup of the parmesan and stir until incorporated. Sprinkle the remaining parmesan over the top. Place the pan under the broiler and broil until the parmesan has melted. Remove from the broiler and garnish with the bread crumbs and chives. Serve immediately.

FRIENDS OF LITTLE PINE

YOLANDI @YOLANDI_EATS_LA

# orecchiette with braised leeks, asparagus, and english peas

Growing up, I thought pasta came in two forms: spaghetti and lasagna. Now I realize there are as many pasta shapes and names as there are stars in the sky, and this particular configuration is now a favorite. I particularly love the way in which it balances the bright snap of asparagus and peas with the reassuring savory yield of the pasta and the leeks.

**TIME:** 45 MINUTES
**SERVES:** 4 TO 6

One 16-ounce box dried orecchiette

2 tablespoons olive oil

3 tablespoons Cultured Butter (page 16)

2 leeks, white part only, rinsed well and cut into half moons

2 garlic cloves, minced

1 teaspoon kosher salt, plus more if needed

½ cup white wine

½ cup water

1 bunch asparagus, tips cut from the stalks, stalks cut into small rounds

1 cup fresh or frozen peas

1 tablespoon fresh lemon juice

⅓ cup coarsely chopped fresh mint, for garnish

Freshly ground black pepper

Shredded vegan parmesan

1  Bring a large pot of water to a boil. Cook the pasta according to the package instructions; drain.

2  In a large sauté pan, heat the olive oil and 1 tablespoon of the butter over medium heat. When the butter has melted, add the leeks and garlic and stir to coat. Season with the salt and sauté for 6 to 8 minutes. Add the wine and cook for 3 to 5 minutes, until it has completely evaporated. Add the water and cook, stirring occasionally, for 3 to 5 minutes, until it has evaporated, then cook for another 7 to 10 minutes, until the leeks are slightly caramelized and completely soft. Add the asparagus stalks and tips and cook for about 3 minutes, until just tender. Add the peas and toss to coat. Once the peas are tender, add the pasta to the pan and stir to combine. Add the remaining 2 tablespoons butter and the lemon juice and toss to fully incorporate all the ingredients. Taste and adjust the seasoning if needed. Transfer to serving bowls and garnish with the mint, freshly ground black pepper, and parmesan.

# gnocchi in white wine cream sauce with shiitakes and almond ricotta

The three-year-old daughter of a friend of mine recently described gnocchi as "little pillows," which made me think that she'll either grow up to be a poet or a food critic. Or both. In this indulgent recipe—our most beloved gnocchi dish of many iterations over the years—the gnocchi are extravagantly crowned with crisp shiitake, a decadent white wine cream sauce, and housemade ricotta.

**TIME:** 2 HOURS

**SERVES:** 6 (10 PIECES EACH)

### GNOCCHI

1¼ pounds Idaho potatoes

2 tablespoons brown flaxseeds

1 cup distilled water

2 tablespoons very thinly sliced fresh basil leaves

1½ teaspoons minced garlic

½ teaspoon kosher salt

1¼ cups unbleached all-purpose flour, plus more if needed

### WHITE WINE CREAM SAUCE

¼ cup olive oil

¼ cup finely diced shallot

2 tablespoons minced garlic

¼ cup chickpea flour

¾ cup white wine

4 cups Cashew Cream (page 18)

1 teaspoon kosher salt

¼ teaspoon freshly ground white pepper

### ASSEMBLY

Salt

3 tablespoons extra-virgin olive oil

1 cup cremini mushrooms, stemmed and thinly sliced

1 cup shiitake mushrooms, stemmed and thinly sliced

6 tablespoons Almond Ricotta (page 20), for serving

½ cup Shiitake Crisp (page 41), for garnish

¼ cup chopped fresh parsley leaves, for garnish

Freshly ground black pepper

**1  MAKE THE GNOCCHI:** Put the unpeeled potatoes in a large pot. Fill the pot with enough cold water to cover the potatoes by at least 2 inches and bring to a simmer over medium-high heat. Reduce the heat to medium, partially cover the pot, and simmer the potatoes for 30 to 35 minutes, until they are completely tender and easily pierced with a skewer. Drain the potatoes and allow them to cool completely. Peel the skin off the potatoes. Grate potatoes on a box grater using the smallest side.

**2**  Bring the water to a boil in a small pot. Add the flaxseeds and stir. Boil the seeds for 5 to 7 minutes. Strain the mixture through a fine-mesh strainer into a bowl; discard the seeds. Set aside 2 tablespoons of the flax gel to use in the gnocchi. (Store the remainder in an airtight container in the refrigerator for up to 1 week or in the freezer indefinitely.)

**3**  In a large bowl, combine the potatoes, basil, 1 tablespoon of the flax gel, the garlic, and salt and mix with your hands until thoroughly combined.

RECIPE CONTINUES ➜

Add the flour and mix until a dough forms. If the dough is too sticky, sprinkle it with more flour. If the dough is too crumbly and not coming together, add a little more of the flax gel.

4  Form the dough into small balls about 1 centimeter wide. Place a dough ball at the widest part of a fork and, with the side of your thumb, gently press down halfway. Roll the flattened dough over itself to form a small cavity on one side of the gnocchi (see photo). Continue rolling the gnocchi toward the tip of the fork until it rolls off. The gnocchi will be a little bit too tall, so press it down slightly to get it back to the width of the fork. Repeat with the remaining balls of dough. The gnocchi can be refrigerated on a sheet pan, wrapped in plastic wrap, until ready to use.

5  **MAKE THE WHITE WINE CREAM SAUCE:** In a large saucepan, heat the olive oil over medium heat. Add the shallot and garlic and cook for 3 to 5 minutes, until soft. Add the chickpea flour and cook, stirring, for 2 to 3 minutes, until the flour starts to brown slightly. Add the wine and stir, scraping up any browned bits from the bottom of the pan, then whisk well until the wine is fully incorporated and cook for 5 to 7 minutes, until reduced by half. The mixture will be quite thick. Add the cashew cream, salt, and pepper. Simmer, whisking continuously, for 10 minutes, until the sauce is thick and creamy. Transfer the sauce to a high-speed blender and blend until smooth; set aside.

6  **TO ASSEMBLE:** Bring a large pot of salted water to a boil. In a large pan, heat 1 tablespoon of the olive oil over high heat. Add the cremini and shiitake mushrooms to the pan. Sauté until cooked, then add the sauce and stir to combine. Reduce the heat to low to keep warm.

7  When the water is boiling, add the gnocchi in batches and cook for about 1 minute, until they float to the surface. Lift the gnocchi from the pot with a slotted spoon and transfer to a large plate or tray in a single layer. Repeat to cook the remaining gnocchi. Let cool. Drizzle the cooled gnocchi with 1 tablespoon of the olive oil. Toss gently with your hands to coat.

8  When you are ready to serve the gnocchi, in a large skillet, heat the remaining 1 tablespoon olive oil over medium heat. Add the gnocchi and fry for about 30 seconds on each side, until golden brown and crisp. Divide the sauce among six serving bowls. Place the gnocchi on top (about 10 pieces per bowl) and scatter about 1 tablespoon of the almond ricotta over each serving. Garnish with the shiitake crisp and parsley. Grind a small amount of pepper on top and serve.

# sausage and polenta

This dish offers a refined spin on polenta, an Italian classic, which serves as a natural base for any number of savory dishes. Here, we've paired it with our housemade fennel sausage and legendary marinara, then topped it with fresh basil and cherry tomatoes. Finish it with your favorite vegan parmesan and serve it at dinner parties or family gatherings—it's a fail-proof, crowd-pleasing comfort food.

**TIME:** 2 HOURS

**SERVES:** 4 TO 6

½ teaspoon kosher salt

¾ cup quick-cooking polenta

Nonstick cooking spray

4 cups Tomato Sauce (page 40)

4 tablespoons olive oil

1 Italian Sausage (page 45), cut into ¾-inch-thick rounds

1 cup grated vegan parmesan, for serving

10 fresh basil leaves, thinly sliced, for garnish

10 grape tomatoes, cut in half

1 In a medium pot, bring 2¼ cups water and the salt to a boil. Add the polenta and cook, stirring continuously, for 3 to 4 minutes. Reduce the heat to low and cook, stirring every 5 to 6 minutes, for 20 minutes more. Spray a 6 × 9-inch baking sheet liberally with nonstick spray and transfer the polenta to the baking sheet. Smooth out the polenta to make the thickness as even as possible. Refrigerate for 30 minutes, or until set.

2 Remove the polenta from the refrigerator and turn it upside down onto a cutting board. Cut the polenta in half lengthwise, then cut each half in half again lengthwise; you should now have four long pieces. Cut each of those in half again.

3 In a medium saucepan, warm the tomato sauce over medium heat.

4 In a large skillet, heat 3 tablespoons of the olive oil over a medium heat. Add the polenta and sear on each side until golden brown. Set the polenta aside. If the pan looks dry, add the remaining 1 tablespoon olive oil and heat over medium heat. Add the sausage and cook for 2 to 3 minutes per side, until crisp.

5 You have a couple of options for plating this dish: You can divide the sauce among four bowls and arrange two pieces of the polenta and three or four pieces of the sausage in each bowl, topping them with the parmesan, basil, and tomatoes. Or you can serve the components separately for a family-style approach.

# rigatoni arrabbiata

This pasta dish comes with one small caveat: it's a little bit spicy. For most people, it's just the right amount of spice, but for a few of our delicate friends, it's just too fiery. (Fun fact: *Arrabbiata* translates as "angry.") The dish is also rich and hearty and—I say this as a recovering alcoholic—addictive. You could always leave out, or cut back on, the red pepper flakes, but as some exercise guru in the '80s first said, "No pain, no gain."

**TIME:** 45 MINUTES

**SERVES:** 4

16 ounces dried penne pasta

5 tablespoons olive oil

2 garlic cloves, minced

One 14-ounce can crushed tomatoes

1 tablespoon tomato paste

½ teaspoon red pepper flakes, or more to taste

1 cup finely crumbled Italian Sausage (page 45)

½ teaspoon sea salt

4 cups loosely packed arugula

½ cup shredded vegan parmesan, for serving

6 fresh basil leaves, thinly sliced, for garnish

1  Bring a large pot of water to a boil. Cook the penne according to the package instructions. Drain the penne, transfer to a bowl, and toss with 2 tablespoons of the olive oil. Set aside.

2  In a medium saucepan, heat the remaining 3 tablespoons olive oil over medium-high heat. Add the garlic and sauté for 2 to 3 minutes, until aromatic. Add the crushed tomatoes, tomato paste, and red pepper flakes. Reduce the heat to low and cook, stirring gently, for 4 minutes. Raise the heat to medium and add the sausage. Simmer for 8 minutes, until the sauce has reduced slightly. Remove from the heat, season with the salt, and stir in the arugula. Add the pasta to the sauce and toss to coat evenly.

3  Transfer the pasta and sauce to a serving bowl and top liberally with the parmesan. Garnish with the basil and serve.

# panko-crusted piccata

One of the goals in opening Little Pine was to serve food that even nonvegans could love. We came up with this panko-crusted piccata, paired with garlic mashed potatoes and savory "butter," as something decadent for vegans but more specifically for their nonvegan friends. It's still profoundly gratifying to watch anxious omnivores bite into this and realize that they actually like vegan food . . .

**TIME:** 2 HOURS

**SERVES:** 5

## SEITAN "CHICKEN BREASTS"

1½ cups vital wheat gluten, plus more for dusting

1¼ cups soft or silken tofu, drained and crumbled

2 tablespoons water

2 tablespoons Broth Powder (page 35)

2 teaspoons kosher salt

1 teaspoon onion powder

1 teaspoon garlic powder

Nonstick cooking spray

## GARLIC BUTTER CAPER SAUCE

½ cup Garlic Butter (page 17)

1 cup dry white wine

1 tablespoon fresh lemon juice

2 tablespoons capers

Salt and freshly ground black pepper

## SEITAN CHICKEN BREADING

½ cup plus 2 tablespoons unbleached all-purpose flour

2 teaspoons garlic powder

2 teaspoons onion powder

2 teaspoons kosher salt

1 cup Cashew Cream (page 18)

2 teaspoons sriracha

2 teaspoons fresh lemon juice

¼ cup canola oil, for frying

2 cups panko bread crumbs

—

1 recipe Garlic Mashed Potatoes (page 135), for serving

¼ cup fresh flat-leaf parsley, coarsely chopped, for garnish

1 teaspoon red pepper flakes, for garnish

**1 MAKE THE SEITAN "CHICKEN BREASTS":** In a food processor, combine the vital wheat gluten, tofu, water, broth powder, salt, onion powder, and garlic powder. Pulse until the ingredients are well combined and the dough forms a ball. Be careful not to overwork the dough or the seitan will become chewy.

**2** Lightly dust a clean work surface with some vital wheat gluten. Place the dough ball on the surface and lightly dust the top of it. (The dough will be sticky and the dusting of vital wheat gluten will help it not stick to your hands.) Cut the dough into 5 pieces. Carefully stretch and form the dough into oval shapes about 5 × 6 inches.

**3** Fill a large pot with about 3 inches of water and bring the water to a simmer. Lightly spray a steamer basket with nonstick spray and place it inside the pot. Lay the seitan chicken in the steamer basket carefully, trying not to let the pieces overlap. If they do, spray them with nonstick spray to keep them from sticking together. (You can steam the seitan in two batches if your steamer basket is small.) Cover and steam for 25 minutes, flipping the seitan chicken pieces halfway through so they steam evenly. The seitan will double in size and lighten in color. Keep the water at a simmer and be careful not to turn the heat up too high, as this can result in the seitan being chewy. Remove the seitan from the steamer basket and let cool until room temperature. Refrigerate for about 1 hour.

**4** **MAKE THE GARLIC BUTTER CAPER SAUCE:** In a medium saucepan, melt the garlic butter over medium heat. Add the wine and cook for 3 to 5 minutes, until reduced by half. Add the lemon juice and capers, raise the heat to medium-high, and bring to a simmer. Season the sauce with salt and pepper. Remove from the heat and set aside.

**5** **BREAD AND FRY THE SEITAN CHICKEN:** In a medium bowl, whisk together the flour, garlic powder, onion powder, and salt. In a 4-cup pitcher or bowl, whisk together the cashew cream, sriracha, and lemon juice. Slowly pour the wet ingredients into the dry ingredients and whisk thoroughly until no lumps remain.

**6** In a medium saucepan, heat the oil over medium-high heat. Line a plate with paper towels and set it nearby.

**7** Place the panko on a plate. Add the seitan chicken pieces to the bowl with the batter, turning them to coat generously. Remove one piece of the seitan chicken from the batter, letting any excess drip off, then dredge it in the panko to coat, making sure to pack it firmly against the seitan chicken so it is evenly coated. Gently place the panko-coated seitan chicken in the hot oil and fry for 3 to 5 minutes, until golden, then flip and fry for another 3 to 5 minutes, until golden on the second side. Transfer the fried seitan chicken to the paper towel–lined plate. Repeat to bread and fry the remaining pieces of seitan chicken.

**8** Place a mound of the garlic mashed potatoes at the center of each plate. Cut each piece of seitan chicken in half and position the halves on top of the potatoes. Top with the sauce and garnish with the parsley and red pepper flakes.

# mushroom potpie

The stars of this dish are the king trumpet mushrooms, which are so revered as a meat substitute that our chef likes to call them "planet-savers." They're not just filler, either, but rather have a complex umami flavor and are rich in protein, vitamin $B_6$, fiber, and antioxidants. In combination with veggies such as peas, carrots, and celery, and smothered in a white gravy, these mushrooms play a central role in creating a dish that debunks the notion that vegan food fails to be filling. It's hearty enough to satisfy the hungriest mouths at your table—and those who favor meat-centric dishes, too.

**TIME:** 2 HOURS

**SERVES:** 6

## PIE DOUGH

2¼ cups plus 2 tablespoons unbleached all-purpose flour, plus more for dusting

½ teaspoon sugar

¾ teaspoon kosher salt

2 cups Hard Butter (page 14), cubed and chilled

¼ cup cold water

## PIE FILLING

8 king trumpet mushrooms

4 tablespoons olive oil

1 white onion, finely diced

2 cups diced carrots

1 cup diced celery

3 garlic cloves, finely chopped

3 tablespoons unbleached all-purpose flour

1 cup dry white wine

2 cups vegetable stock

½ cup Cashew Cream (page 18) or unsweetened unflavored nondairy milk of your choice

1 tablespoon tamari

2 teaspoons Broth Powder (page 35)

2 teaspoons minced fresh thyme

1 teaspoon minced fresh rosemary

1 teaspoon finely chopped fresh sage

2 bay leaves

½ cup fresh or frozen peas

½ teaspoon sea salt, plus more if needed

¼ teaspoon freshly ground black pepper, plus more if needed

—

¼ cup unsweetened soy milk, for brushing

**1 MAKE THE PIE DOUGH:** In the bowl of a stand mixer fitted with the paddle attachment, mix together the flour, sugar, and salt. On low speed, add the butter and mix until it breaks down into pieces the size of hazelnuts. With the mixer running, slowly stream in the cold water and mix until the dough is just combined; do not overmix.

**2** On a floured surface, pat the dough into a rectangle. With one long side facing you, fold the right third of the dough over the center third of the dough, then fold the remaining third of the dough over the center. Pat the dough into a round and wrap tightly in plastic wrap. Refrigerate for at least 30 minutes before using, and store refrigerated for up to 1 week.

**3 MEANWHILE, MAKE THE PIE FILLING:** Wipe any dirt from the mushrooms. Lay them on a flat surface and, with a fork, shred the mushroom stems and caps into pieces. In a large skillet, heat 2 tablespoons of the olive oil over medium heat. Add the mushrooms and sauté for 10 to 15 minutes, until soft and lightly caramelized in places. Remove from the heat and set aside.

**4** Preheat the oven to 350°F.

RECIPE CONTINUES →

# spinach and mushroom crepes

In our savory crepe, spinach is paired with mushrooms and smothered in our decadent housemade cheese sauce—because a savory crepe without (vegan) *fromage* is like a water park without water.

**TIME:** 45 MINUTES

**SERVES:** 3

## CREPES

2 cups chickpea flour

2 cups water

¼ cup olive oil

1 tablespoon minced fresh rosemary

1 teaspoon kosher salt

1 teaspoon freshly ground black pepper

## SPINACH AND MUSHROOM FILLING

2 tablespoons olive oil

1 garlic clove, minced

8 cups baby spinach

2 cups sliced cremini mushrooms

1 teaspoon kosher salt

3 cups Cheese Sauce (page 36)

1 cup grated vegan parmesan

—

5 basil leaves, thinly sliced, for garnish

**1 MAKE THE CREPES:** In a medium bowl, whisk together the chickpea flour, water, olive oil, rosemary, salt, and pepper until combined and no lumps remain. Let the batter rest at room temperature for 30 minutes.

**2** Heat a 12-inch nonstick crepe pan over medium heat. Pour ¾ cup of the batter into the hot pan and spread it evenly with a crepe spreader. Cook for 1 to 2 minutes, until the crepe is golden, then loosen the crepe with a spatula and turn over, cooking until golden on the second side. Transfer the crepe to a plate and repeat with the remaining batter. Set the crepes aside.

**3 MAKE THE SPINACH AND MUSHROOM FILLING:** In a medium saucepan, heat the olive oil over medium heat. Add the garlic and sauté, stirring, for 2 minutes, until fragrant. Add the spinach, mushrooms, and salt. Cook for 3 to 4 minutes, until the mushrooms are soft and the spinach has wilted. Add the cheese sauce and parmesan and stir until piping-hot.

**4** Place a crepe on a plate. Spread one-third of the filling down the middle. Gently fold both sides of the crepe over on top of each other. Flip the crepe over so that the fold is on the bottom. Repeat to fill the remaining crepes. Garnish with the basil and serve.

# stuffed shells with basil tofu ricotta

Before we opened Little Pine, I told our staff that one of my favorite foods growing up was stuffed shells, and that I had sorely missed them since becoming a vegan. They heard my thinly veiled plea and used their knowledge and creativity to make stuffed shells that are every bit as good as those my mom used to make. When people have asked me in the past about the creamy ricotta in this recipe, I've always said, "I don't know how they do it," so I'm excited to share the secret at last.

**TIME:** 1 HOUR 30 MINUTES
**SERVES:** 4

One 12-ounce package jumbo pasta shells (about 24)

2 tablespoons olive oil

**BASIL TOFU RICOTTA**

2 garlic cloves, coarsely chopped

1 teaspoon kosher salt

3 tablespoons nutritional yeast

3 tablespoons fresh lemon juice

One 14-ounce block extra-firm tofu, drained and crumbled

⅓ cup fresh basil leaves, thinly sliced, plus more for garnish

—

1 recipe Tomato Sauce (page 40)

½ cup shredded vegan parmesan

**1** Preheat the oven to 350°F.

**2** Bring a large pot of water to a boil. Cook the shells according to the package instructions. Drain the shells well, rinse under cold water, and return them to the pot. Add the olive oil and toss to coat so that the shells do not stick together. Set aside.

**3** **MAKE THE BASIL TOFU RICOTTA:** In a food processor, combine the garlic, salt, nutritional yeast, and lemon juice and process until smooth. Add the crumbled tofu and process until completely smooth. Transfer the mixture to a medium bowl and stir in the basil.

**4** To assemble, evenly spread about 2 cups of the tomato sauce over the bottom of a large casserole dish. Scoop about 2 tablespoons of the tofu ricotta into each shell and place them open side up in the casserole dish. Repeat until all the ricotta has been used up. Pour the remaining tomato sauce on top of the stuffed shells. Bake for 25 minutes. Top with the parmesan and bake until the cheese is melted and lightly browned. Serve piping-hot, scattered with fresh basil.

# trumpet mushroom "scallops"

I've never had a "real" scallop, but I think it's pretty amazing that using plants, you can make a scallop that's better for the environment, has the healing magic of mushrooms, and allows cute little sea creatures to "just keep swimming/floating/holding on to rocks." Sometimes being a gluten-free person is tough when you're vegan—I love gluten, and I'm sad for those who can't have it—but this dish is sort of the perfect solution. Plus, it's fancy, and your friends/lover/spouse/pet pig will be impressed!

**AHEAD:** MARINATE MUSHROOMS OVERNIGHT AND SOAK CASHEWS FOR 6 HOURS

**TIME:** 1 HOUR 30 MINUTES (PLUS MARINATING AND SOAKING TIME)

**SERVES:** 4

### GARLIC CASHEW CREAM

6 garlic cloves, peeled

2 tablespoons olive oil, plus more for drizzling

1 cup cashews, soaked for 6 hours, then drained

1 tablespoon fresh lemon juice

½ cup water

½ teaspoon kosher salt

### "SCALLOPS"

12 large king trumpet mushrooms

2 cups warm water

1 cup dry white wine

½ teaspoon minced fresh oregano leaves

1 teaspoon minced fresh parsley leaves

2 tablespoons olive oil

2 teaspoons tamari

2 teaspoons Broth Powder (page 35)

Pinch of red pepper flakes

### HERBED QUINOA

1 cup dried quinoa

2 cups water

1 bunch chives, finely chopped

1 bunch flat-leaf parsley, minced

2 tablespoons olive oil

1 tablespoon fresh lemon juice

2 teaspoons kosher salt

—

4 tablespoons Cultured Butter (page 16)

1 lemon, quartered, for serving

1 tablespoon finely chopped fresh chives, for garnish

**1** MAKE THE GARLIC CASHEW CREAM: Preheat the oven to 350°F.

**2** On a baking sheet, drizzle the garlic with olive oil and roast for about 10 minutes, until soft and fragrant. Remove from the oven.

**3** In a high-speed blender, combine the roasted garlic, cashews, olive oil, lemon juice, water, and salt. Blend on high speed, stopping to scrape down the sides as needed, until completely smooth and no lumps remain. Set aside.

**4** MAKE THE "SCALLOPS": Slice the mushroom stems crosswise into 1-inch-thick pieces to make "scallops." Score the tops and bottoms of each scallop. In a large bowl, whisk together the warm water, wine, oregano, parsley, olive oil, tamari, broth powder, and red pepper flakes. Add the scallops and marinate in the refrigerator for at least 1 hour or up to overnight.

RECIPE CONTINUES ➜

# desserts

# strawberry ice cream

I want to write something germane and insightful about our strawberry ice cream, but the best I can come up with is this: It's great. Really. Sometimes complicated is wonderful. And sometimes, as is the case here, we don't need to gild the lily. We can just enjoy a perfect little bowl of vegan strawberry ice cream.

**TIME:** 11 HOURS (INCLUDES CHILLING, CHURNING, AND FREEZING)

**MAKES:** 1 QUART

1 cup hemp milk

1 cup coconut cream

1 cup fresh strawberries, hulled, and coarsely chopped

⅓ cup sugar

1 tablespoon fresh lemon juice

¾ teaspoon pure vanilla extract

⅛ teaspoon kosher salt

½ teaspoon xanthan gum

1  In a high-speed blender, combine the hemp milk, coconut cream, strawberries, sugar, lemon juice, vanilla, salt, and xanthan gum. Blend on high speed for 3 minutes. Pour into an airtight container and refrigerate for at least 8 hours and up to 10 hours.

2  Pour the chilled ice cream base into an ice cream maker and churn according to the manufacturer's instructions. Transfer the ice cream into a 1-quart container, cover, and freeze for at least 2 hours and up to 2 months, until ready to serve.

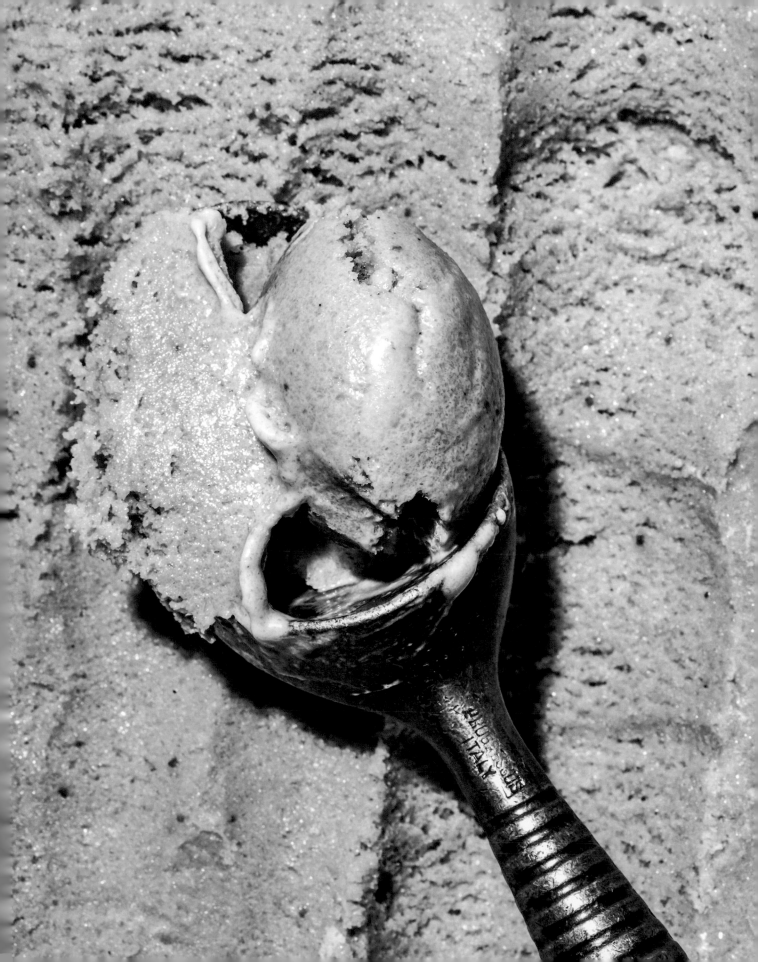

# apple berry crumble

When I was opening Little Pine, I wanted to stay away from including dishes on our menu that looked/tasted/sounded like something I would've seen on a vegan restaurant menu in the late '80s. The one exception is this apple berry crumble; while it sounds like an old hippie dessert (nothing wrong with old hippies, to be clear . . .), it's indulgent in ways that didn't exist in vegan restaurants in 1987. It's also oh so simple in terms of ingredients—take a few dry goods from your pantry and mix them up with fresh apples, berries, and a bit of that magical vegan butter and voilà: a semi-virtuous dessert packed with some of nature's best antioxidants. P.S. It's gluten-free, too.

**TIME:** 45 MINUTES
**SERVES:** 6

**APPLE BERRY FILLING**

2 cups diced apples

1 cup fresh blueberries

1 cup fresh blackberries

1 cup fresh raspberries

1½ teaspoons fresh lemon juice

½ teaspoon pure vanilla extract

¼ cup sugar

3 tablespoons cornstarch

¼ teaspoon kosher salt

**GLUTEN-FREE STREUSEL**

5 tablespoons gluten-free all-purpose flour

1 cup blanched almond flour

¾ cup sugar

¾ teaspoon kosher salt

5 tablespoons Hard Butter (page 14), chopped into small cubes and chilled

—

Ice cream or Coconut Whipped Cream (page 22), for serving

1  Preheat the oven to 350°F.

2  **MAKE THE APPLE BERRY FILLING:** In a medium sauté pan, dry sauté the apples over medium heat for 8 to 10 minutes, until softened. Transfer the apples to a large bowl and add the blueberries, blackberries, raspberries, lemon juice, and vanilla; toss to combine.

3  In a small bowl, whisk together the sugar, cornstarch, and salt. Add the sugar mixture to the berry mixture and fold together until evenly distributed.

4  **MAKE THE GLUTEN-FREE STREUSEL:** In the bowl of a stand mixer fitted with the paddle attachment, mix together the gluten-free flour, almond flour, sugar, and salt until combined. With the mixer on low speed, start to add the butter a little at a time and mix until a crumbly dough forms.

5  Pour ¾ cup of the apple berry filling into each of six 6-ounce ramekins. Top each ramekin with ⅓ cup of the streusel.

6  Bake for 20 to 25 minutes until the streusel is browned and the berry mixture starts to bubble. Remove from the oven and let cool briefly before serving. Serve à la mode or topped with a dollop of coconut whipped cream.

# chocolate chip cookies

I was reading an interview with Common, the rapper/actor/activist, wherein he said that our Little Pine chocolate chip cookies were one of his favorite things. This made me love Common even more, especially for his clearly evolved and unimpeachable taste in cookies. Really, though—and I can say this without being a braggart as I didn't invent this recipe—these are probably the best vegan chocolate chip cookies in town/in the country/in the world/in this solar system. When made right, they should be alternately gooey and crisp in all the right places. Serve with napkins, because . . . chocolate. P.S. Adding Vanilla Bean Ice Cream (page 225) is encouraged.

**TIME:** 1 HOUR
**MAKES:** 18 COOKIES

10 tablespoons Hard Butter (page 14)

¾ cup lightly packed light brown sugar

½ cup granulated sugar

1½ teaspoons kosher salt

¾ teaspoon pure vanilla extract

4½ teaspoons Bob's Red Mill Egg Replacer

¼ cup plus 1½ teaspoons water

1¼ cups unbleached all-purpose flour

¾ teaspoon baking soda

1¼ cups vegan dark chocolate chips

**1** Preheat the oven to 350°F. Line two 9 × 13-inch baking sheets with parchment paper.

**2** In the bowl of a stand mixer fitted with the paddle attachment, mix together the butter, brown sugar, granulated sugar, and salt on low speed until creamy but not whipped. In a small bowl, whisk together the vanilla extract, egg replacer, and water. Add to the butter mixture and mix until combined.

**3** Sift the flour and baking soda into the mixer bowl. Start to pulse the mixture while slowly adding in the chocolate chips until the dough comes together.

**4** Using a 1½-ounce cookie scoop, scoop the cookie dough onto the prepared baking sheets, spacing the cookies 1 inch apart. Refrigerate the cookies for 30 minutes.

**5** Bake for 8 to 10 minutes, until the edges are golden brown. Leave on the baking sheet until completely cooled. Store the cookies, covered, at room temperature for up to 4 days.

# baked alaska

This dessert originated in my birthplace, New York City, to commemorate the purchase of Alaska from Russia, which ultimately gave us Sarah Palin but also lots of nature and a place to maybe move when climate change renders Los Angeles unlivable. So, on balance, I think it's worth celebrating with this fancy-looking ice cream cake that otherwise has nothing to do with the forty-ninth state (except that it's frozen?). This isn't the easiest recipe, but the reward for your labor is getting to torch the cake at the end, which is a really fun way to take out any aggressions you may have. Although, to be clear, using fire to release aggression is generally not such a great idea.

**TIME:** 6 HOURS (INCLUDING FREEZING TIME)

**SERVES:** 8

## VANILLA CAKE

Nonstick cooking spray

¾ cup plus 2 tablespoons unbleached all-purpose flour

1 teaspoon baking powder

½ teaspoon Bob's Red Mill Egg Replacer

⅛ teaspoon kosher salt

¼ cup plus 1½ teaspoons unsweetened soy milk

3 tablespoons water

2 teaspoons pure vanilla extract

½ cup Hard Butter (page 14), at room temperature

¼ cup sugar

## CANDIED RICE CEREAL

¼ cup sugar

1 tablespoon water

1 tablespoon corn syrup

1½ teaspoons Hard Butter (page 14)

¼ teaspoon baking soda

⅛ teaspoon kosher salt

Scant 2 cups crisp rice cereal

## TO ASSEMBLE

Nonstick cooking spray

4 cups Strawberry Ice Cream (page 198)

1½ cups Fudge Sauce (page 25), at room temperature

3 cups Chickpea Meringue (page 22)

**1  MAKE THE VANILLA CAKE:** Preheat the oven to 350°F. Spray an 8-inch round cake pan with nonstick spray and line the bottom with a round of parchment paper cut to fit.

**2**  In a medium bowl, whisk together the flour, baking powder, egg replacer, and salt. In a liquid measuring cup, combine the soy milk, water, and vanilla. In the bowl of a stand mixer fitted with the paddle attachment, cream together the butter and sugar. Alternate adding the flour mixture and soy milk mixture, starting with the flour mixture and scraping down the bowl after each addition, and mix until a smooth batter forms.

**3**  Pour the batter into the prepared pan. Bake for 22 to 25 minutes, until the top of the cake springs back when touched. Remove from the oven and let cool in the pan for 10 minutes and then transfer to a cooling rack to cool completely.

**4  MEANWHILE, MAKE THE CANDIED RICE CEREAL:** Line a baking sheet with parchment paper.

RECIPE CONTINUES ➜

**5**  In a medium pot, combine the sugar, water, and corn syrup and heat over medium heat, stirring, until the sugar has dissolved, then cook, stirring gently, for 2 to 3 minutes, until the mixture is golden. Carefully add the butter, baking soda, and salt, then add the rice cereal and stir to coat; work quickly to prevent burning. Remove from the heat. Scrape the coated cereal onto the prepared baking sheet and carefully spread it out into an even layer. Set aside to cool. Once cooled, break the candied rice cereal apart into small pieces.

**6**  ASSEMBLE THE BAKED ALASKA: Spray a 5-cup metal bowl with nonstick spray and line it with plastic wrap. Pack the bottom of the bowl with the strawberry ice cream and freeze for 2 hours to set. Pour the fudge sauce on top of the ice cream and freeze for 1 hour more. Crumble the candied rice cereal on top of the fudge, then top with the vanilla cake round, pressing down gently but firmly so the cake adheres to the candied cereal layer evenly. Freeze until the ice cream is hard, at least 2 hours and up to 1 month.

**7**  Invert the bowl onto a cake board or cake stand and carefully remove the bowl. With a spatula, smooth and swirl the meringue over the dessert and brown the meringue with a kitchen torch. Serve immediately.

# cantaloupe sorbet

I'm protective of the modest cantaloupe, which has for years been maligned as a filler fruit, trotted out at generic hotel brunches and easily ignored on fruit platters. In fact, it's a refreshing summer treat packed with nutrients such as beta-carotene, vitamin C, potassium, and fiber. It's honestly no less nutritious as sorbet, either, save for a bit of added sugar. If I were the type of person who stocked my freezer with desserts, I'd make sure to have this on hand through the increasingly scorching Angeleno summers, during which it'd offer pitch-perfect, guilt-free relief from the heat.

**TIME:** 11 HOURS (INCLUDES CHILLING, CHURNING, AND FREEZING)

**MAKES:** ABOUT 3½ CUPS

2½ cups cubed cantaloupe

1 cup water

½ cup Vanilla Syrup (page 28)

¼ teaspoon kosher salt

2½ teaspoons fruit pectin

1  In a high-speed blender, combine the cantaloupe, water, simple syrup, and salt. Blend on high speed for 5 minutes, or until smooth. Transfer the mixture to a small pot and whisk in the fruit pectin. Bring the mixture to a simmer over medium-low heat, stirring occasionally, then remove from the heat. Pour into an airtight container and let cool completely, then refrigerate for at least 8 hours.

2  Pour the chilled sorbet base into an ice cream maker and churn according to the manufacturer's instructions. Transfer the churned sorbet to a freezer-safe 1-quart container, cover, and freeze for at least 2 hours and up to 2 months before serving.

# butterscotch pudding

I will be forever grateful our pastry chef figured out how to make this traditionally dairy-heavy dessert sans milk, eggs, or butter. The necessary modifications have a welcome consequence, too, which is that this vegan version is lighter and healthier than the dish from which it derives inspiration. A diner once told me it was "the best thing [she'd] ever tasted," which is, simply, the nicest thing you can hear when you own a restaurant.

**TIME:** 8 HOURS 45 MINUTES (INCLUDES CHILLING TIME)

**SERVES:** 4

## BUTTERSCOTCH PUDDING

2½ cups coconut milk

3 tablespoons plus 1½ teaspoons cornstarch

1¼ teaspoons pure vanilla extract

⅛ teaspoon kosher salt

1 tablespoon Hard Butter (page 14)

1 cup packed brown sugar

## PECAN CRUMBLE TOPPING

1 cup unbleached all-purpose flour

⅓ cup firmly packed brown sugar

½ teaspoon ground cinnamon

¼ cup ground nutmeg

½ cup chopped pecans

½ cup Hard Butter (page 14), melted

—

½ cup Coconut Whipped Cream (page 22), for serving

**1  MAKE THE BUTTERSCOTCH PUDDING:** In a small bowl, whisk together 1¼ cups of the coconut milk, the cornstarch, vanilla, and salt to make a slurry. In a medium pot, melt the butter over medium-low heat. Add the brown sugar. Slowly stir in the remaining 1¼ cups coconut milk and bring to a simmer. Slowly whisk the slurry into the pot and cook, stirring vigorously, until bubbling and thick. Remove from the heat and let cool completely. Transfer the pudding to an airtight container, press a layer of plastic wrap directly against the surface of the pudding, cover, and refrigerate for at least 8 hours and up to 1 week.

**2  MAKE THE PECAN CRUMBLE TOPPING:** Preheat the oven to 350°F. Line a baking sheet with parchment paper.

**3**  In a medium bowl, combine the flour, brown sugar, cinnamon, and nutmeg. Stir in the pecans, then carefully stir in the melted butter until combined. Spread the mixture evenly over the prepared baking sheet. Bake for 15 to 20 minutes, stirring every 5 minutes, until lightly browned. Let cool completely and store in an airtight container in the refrigerator until ready to use, or up to 1 week.

**4**  Portion the chilled butterscotch pudding evenly among four bowls. Crumble about ¼ cup of the pecan topping onto each bowl and top with a dollop of coconut whipped cream, then serve.

# mini chocolate pecan cheesecakes

**AHEAD:** SOAK CASHEWS OVERNIGHT

**TIME:** 9 HOURS (INCLUDES CHILLING TIME PLUS SOAKING OVERNIGHT)

**MAKES:** 12 MINI CHEESECAKES

Nonstick cooking spray

¾ cup Gluten-Free Graham Cracker Crust Mix (page 23)

1 recipe Chocolate Pecan cheesecake filling (page 211)

2 cups Chickpea Meringue (page 22)

½ cup Fudge Sauce (page 25)

**1** Preheat the oven to 350°F. Lightly oil a 12-cup mini cheesecake pan with removable bottoms.

**2** Place 1 tablespoon of the graham cracker crust mix in the well of each cheesecake pan. Firmly press the crust down in an even layer using a tamper or shot glass.

**3** Bake for 12 minutes, until the crust is slightly darker in color. Remove from the oven and let cool completely.

**4** Divide the cheesecake filling evenly among the cheesecake pans. Do not worry if you overfill them slightly. When all of the wells are full, carefully smooth the tops of the cheesecakes using an offset spatula. Place in the refrigerator for at least 8 hours, until completely set.

**5** To serve, gently remove each cheesecake from the pan. Place the cheesecake on a plate and top with a generous spoonful of the chickpea meringue. Using a kitchen torch, toast the meringue until golden brown. Drizzle with the fudge sauce and enjoy.

FRIENDS OF LITTLE PINE

TINY CHEF @THETINYCHEFSHOW

# banana cream pie

If I were to create new words, I'd come up with a way to succinctly describe the look people get in their eyes when they have their first bite of our banana cream pie. It's an expression of rapturous disbelief that makes opening and running a restaurant absolutely worthwhile. Bananas are a bit of a hero/best-kept secret in vegan baking, but rarely does a dessert lean into them so strongly, and to such epic effect. As a result, this is always the dessert I send over to friends' tables to show my appreciation for their patronage of Little Pine.

**TIME:** 5 HOURS (INCLUDES SETTING TIME)

**MAKES:** ONE 9-INCH PIE

Nonstick cooking spray

2 cups Gluten-Free Graham Cracker Crust Mix (page 23)

3 cups unsweetened soy milk

1 vanilla bean, split lengthwise and seeds scraped out

1 cup sugar

6 tablespoons cornstarch

½ teaspoon kosher salt

¼ cup Hard Butter (page 14)

1½ medium bananas, mashed

2 cups Coconut Whipped Cream (page 22)

¼ cup Caramel Sauce (page 25)

1  Preheat the oven to 350°F. Spray a 9-inch pie pan with nonstick spray.

2  Press the graham cracker crust mix into an even layer over the bottom and up the sides of the prepared pan. Bake for 10 minutes until it deepens in color slightly. Remove from the oven and let cool completely.

3  In a medium pot, combine 1 cup of the soy milk and the vanilla bean seeds and bring to a simmer over medium heat.

4  In a medium bowl, whisk together the remaining 2 cups soy milk, the sugar, cornstarch, and salt to make a slurry. Slowly whisk the slurry into the warm soy milk and bring to a boil, stirring continuously. Once the mixture comes to a boil, stir for 1 minute longer, then remove from the heat. Add the butter and mashed bananas and stir to combine.

5  Carefully pour the banana mixture into a blender and blend until very smooth. Pour the banana filling into the pie crust. Refrigerate for at least 4 hours to allow the filling to set.

6  Top the chilled pie with the coconut whipped cream and drizzle with the caramel sauce.

FRIENDS OF LITTLE PINE

BABYCORN THE OPOSSUM @ITSMESESAME

*Ten Little Pine banana cream pies, please!*

# chocolate pecan truffles

While you might be hard-pressed to describe a decadent truffle as "healthy," allow me to sing the praises of the humble pecan: it's packed with antioxidants, protein, fiber, and healthy fats. In other words, you don't need to feel too terribly guilty about eating this, because, well, I said so. For this reason, and because they are delicious, I love to keep these on hand for just a touch of something sweet after dinner. I also usually end dinner parties at my house with a chocolate sampling, and these bite-size treats are the perfect addition to any such offering.

**TIME:** 2 HOURS 30 MINUTES (INCLUDES SETTING TIME)

**MAKES:** 12 TRUFFLES

4½ tablespoons pure maple syrup

4½ tablespoons coconut sugar

½ cup plus 2 teaspoons unsweetened cocoa powder

½ cup plus 2 tablespoons refined coconut oil, melted

½ cup pecans, chopped

1 teaspoon kosher salt

1 teaspoon pure vanilla extract

**TOPPINGS**

¼ cup coconut sugar

¼ cup pecans, toasted and chopped

1  In a small pot, combine the maple syrup and coconut sugar and heat over low heat, gently stirring, until the coconut sugar has dissolved. Remove from the heat and set aside.

2  In a food processor, combine the cocoa powder, coconut oil, pecans, salt, and vanilla and pulse until evenly distributed. With the food processor running, slowly stream in the coconut sugar mixture until everything is just combined. Do not overprocess.

3  Transfer the mixture to a bowl, cover, and refrigerate until completely chilled, about 2 hours, stirring occasionally to ensure that the coconut oil stays incorporated in the mixture.

4  For the toppings, place the coconut sugar and pecans in separate bowls.

5  Scoop 1-tablespoon portions of the chilled truffle mixture and roll into round balls, setting them on a large plate as you go. Roll the balls in your choice of topping, coconut sugar or pecans. Place back in the refrigerator in an airtight container, separated with parchment paper, until ready to serve, for up to 2 weeks.

# caramel spice ice cream

In the late '80s, a friend asked me, as a new vegan, what I missed from the world of nonvegan food. And the first thing I said was "ice cream." Now, clearly, that is no longer the case, as the world is full of amazing vegan ice cream. And whereas sometimes we want our sweets to be simple and, well, sweet, other times we want sweets that are nuanced and even complicated. This caramel spice ice cream is certainly sweet, but with savory and umami notes attenuating the sweetness. And while it might seem like a perfect winter ice cream, it's also really great when the sun is hot and the streets are melting.

**TIME:** 11 HOURS (INCLUDES CHILLING, CHURNING, AND FREEZING)

**MAKES:** 1 QUART

1¼ cups hemp milk

1¼ cups coconut cream

⅓ cup sugar

1¼ teaspoons pure vanilla extract

1¼ teaspoons ground cinnamon

½ teaspoon xanthan gum

⅛ teaspoon ground nutmeg

⅛ teaspoon ground cloves

⅛ teaspoon kosher salt

½ cup Caramel Sauce (page 25)

1  In a blender, combine the hemp milk, coconut cream, sugar, vanilla, cinnamon, xanthan gum, nutmeg, cloves, and salt and blend on high speed for 3 minutes. Pour into an airtight container and refrigerate for at least 8 hours.

2  Pour the chilled ice cream base into an ice cream maker and churn according to the manufacturer's instructions. Transfer the churned ice cream to a freezer-safe 1-quart container and carefully fold in the caramel sauce. You do not want to mix the caramel sauce completely with the ice cream—aim to have ribbons of caramel running throughout. Cover the container and freeze for at least 2 hours, and up to 1 month, before serving.

# chocolate bread pudding

Given that traditional bread pudding draws its rich flavor from milk, cream, butter, and eggs, I think this vegan version is a twenty-first-century marvel. According to our talented pastry chef, this is a dessert that is easily thrown together from the contents of your pantry, and it's also a great way to reduce food waste by transforming stale bread into an indulgence. You don't have to serve this dish with vanilla ice cream, but you probably should . . . or so say the experts (my friends).

**TIME:** 1 HOUR 15 MINUTES

**SERVES:** 6

¼ cup plus 2 tablespoons sugar

¼ cup cornstarch

¼ teaspoon ground cinnamon

¼ cup water

1½ cups unsweetened soy milk

2 teaspoons pure vanilla extract

3 tablespoons Hard Butter (page 14), melted

½ cup Fudge Sauce (page 25), melted

8 slices day-old bread, cut into ½-inch cubes (no crust)

½ cup vegan dark chocolate chips

¼ cup plus 2 tablespoons pecans, chopped

Vanilla Bean Ice Cream (page 225), for serving

1  In a large bowl, whisk together the sugar, cornstarch, and cinnamon. Slowly stream in the water and the soy milk, whisking continuously. Add the vanilla. Stream in the melted butter and whisk vigorously until combined. Whisk in the fudge sauce. Add the cubed bread, chocolate chips, and pecans and toss until the bread is saturated. Let stand for 30 minutes, stirring occasionally, to allow the bread to absorb more of the liquid.

2  Preheat the oven to 350°F.

3  Divide the bread pudding evenly among six ramekins. Place the ramekins in a deep roasting pan and carefully fill the roasting pan with water to come halfway up the sides of the ramekins, being careful not to get any water inside the ramekins.

4  Bake for 40 to 45 minutes, until the center of each bread pudding is firm and the edges are bubbling. Carefully remove from the oven and remove the ramekins from the roasting pan. Serve warm, à la mode. Any leftover puddings can be covered and stored in the refrigerator for up to 1 week. To reheat, cover with aluminum foil and bake at 325°F for 15 minutes until warmed through.

# chocolate lava cakes

It never ceases to amaze me how humble plants—like the apples used in this recipe—can be transformed into more virtuous versions of the sweets many of us grew up begging our parents to make. One of my favorite things about this particular recipe is that its six servings are basically single cakes you can totally justify eating by yourself. After all, celebrations don't always require other human beings . . . or is that just me?

**TIME:** 1 HOUR

**MAKES:** 6 CAKES

Nonstick cooking spray

¼ cup unsweetened cocoa powder, plus more for dusting

½ cup hemp milk, at room temperature

1 teaspoon fresh lemon juice

2 tablespoons refined coconut oil, melted

½ teaspoon pure vanilla extract

½ cup sugar

½ cup unsweetened applesauce, at room temperature

½ cup unbleached all-purpose flour

½ teaspoon baking powder

½ teaspoon kosher salt

½ cup chopped dark chocolate (70% cacao), melted

30 dark chocolate discs (70% cacao)

6 tablespoons Fudge Sauce (page 25)

6 Candied Orange Twists (page 26)

3 cups Grand Marnier Ice Cream (page 224)

1  Preheat the oven to 350°F. Spray a 6-cavity silicone cupcake pan with nonstick spray and dust each cavity with cocoa powder, then tap out any excess.

2  In a large liquid measuring cup, combine the hemp milk and lemon juice and let stand for 5 minutes, until the milk starts to curdle.

3  In a medium bowl, whisk together the melted coconut oil, vanilla, sugar, applesauce, and hemp milk mixture until foamy.

4  In a small bowl, combine the flour, cocoa powder, baking powder, and salt. Add the dry ingredients to the bowl of wet ingredients and whisk until the lumps are gone. Whisk in the melted chocolate.

5  Using a 2-ounce scoop, fill the cavities of the prepared cupcake pan. Carefully place 5 chocolate discs in the center of the batter in each cavity and gently push down, being mindful not to push the discs to the very bottom. Evenly distribute the remaining batter among the cavities to cover the exposed chocolate discs. Bake for about 20 minutes, until the cakes are slightly firm to the touch.

6  Remove from the oven and let cool in the pan for a few moments before carefully flipping the cakes out onto individual plates. Serve warm, topped with 1 tablespoon of the fudge sauce, a candied orange twist, and a scoop of the Grand Marnier ice cream.

# grand marnier ice cream

As a sober person, I feel a bit weird writing about this boozy ice cream; however, the alcohol cooks off in the process of making it, which makes it okay? In other words, children and teetotalers can happily enjoy this ice cream, sans any buzz but that which comes from sugar. We serve it with our chocolate lava cake, but you can enjoy it however you like.

**TIME:** 11 HOURS (INCLUDES CHILLING, CHURNING, AND FREEZING)

**MAKES:** 1 QUART

1¼ cups coconut cream

½ cup hemp milk

½ cup orange juice

¼ cup Grand Marnier

⅓ cup sugar

1¼ teaspoons pure vanilla extract

½ teaspoon xanthan gum

⅛ teaspoon kosher salt

1  In a medium pot, combine the coconut cream, hemp milk, orange juice, Grand Marnier, and sugar and bring to a boil over medium-high heat. Reduce the heat to maintain a simmer and cook, stirring frequently, for 20 minutes. Remove from the heat and let cool to room temperature.

2  Transfer the coconut milk mixture to a high-speed blender and add the vanilla, xanthan gum, and salt. Blend on high speed for 3 minutes. Pour into an airtight container and refrigerate for at least 8 hours and up to 1 week.

3  Pour the chilled ice cream base into an ice cream maker and churn according to the manufacturer's instructions. Transfer the churned ice cream to a freezer-safe 1-quart container, cover, and freeze for at least 2 hours before serving. Store in the freezer for up to 1 month.

# vanilla bean ice cream

Sometimes you combine hundreds of ingredients and processes to create recipes that are delicious and incredibly complicated. And sometimes you make, and eat, vanilla bean ice cream. It's one of those menu items that's so humble and simple, it's easy to overlook. But sit down and have an unadorned spoonful and notice that even if this is an unassuming dessert, it's still got an amazing, nuanced flavor profile.

**TIME:** 11 HOURS (INCLUDES CHILLING, CHURNING, AND FREEZING)

**MAKES:** 1 QUART

1½ cups coconut cream

1 cup hemp milk

⅓ cup sugar

1 vanilla bean, split lengthwise and seeds scraped

1½ teaspoons pure vanilla extract

½ teaspoon xanthan gum

⅛ teaspoon kosher salt

1  In a blender, combine the coconut cream, hemp milk, sugar, vanilla seeds, vanilla extract, xanthan gum, and salt and blend on high speed for 3 minutes. Pour into an airtight container and refrigerate for at least 8 hours.

2  Pour the chilled ice cream base into an ice cream maker and churn according to the manufacturer's instructions. Transfer the ice cream to a freezer-safe 1-quart container, cover, and freeze for at least 2 hours and up to 2 months before serving.

# drinks

# strawberry mint lemonade

This nonalcoholic beverage is simple summertime perfection (although technically, given its use of frozen strawberries, it could be enjoyed year-round—and anyway, the world is only getting warmer!). I envision it served at a large family picnic or, if you're more the introverted type, a party of one spent whiling away a hot afternoon with a good old-fashioned book.

**TIME:** 10 MINUTES

**SERVES:** 8

4 cups frozen strawberries

1 cup fresh lemon juice

1 cup Strawberry Syrup (page 29)

5 cups water

Handful of fresh mint

In a blender, combine the strawberries, lemon juice, strawberry syrup, water, and mint. Blend until fully combined. Strain through a fine-mesh strainer into a pitcher. Serve and enjoy.

# hibiscus mimosa

The hibiscus mimosa is lovely in its simplicity, a beautiful mix of prosecco and hibiscus that begs for a toast (or to be served alongside toast, at brunch). Sub in a nonalcoholic sparkling wine for kids and teetotalers.

**TIME:** 3 MINUTES

**SERVES:** 1

⅓ cup dried hibiscus flowers

⅓ cup sugar

1 lemon wedge

Prosecco

½ ounce hibiscus syrup (from one 8.8-ounce jar of hibiscus flowers in syrup)

½ ounce fresh lemon juice

Hibiscus flower (from one 8.8-ounce jar of hibiscus flowers in syrup), for garnish

1 Combine the hibiscus flowers and sugar in a food processor. Pulse until the flowers are pulverized. (Be certain to use the pulse method to ensure the sugar doesn't melt or heat up.) Pour the hibiscus sugar onto a small plate. Rub the rim of a champagne flute with the lemon wedge. Dip the rim in the hibiscus sugar and twist it to coat.

2 Fill the rimmed champagne flute halfway with prosecco, making certain to tilt the glass when pouring the prosecco to ensure the liquid does not overflow. Add the hibiscus syrup and lemon juice; stir with a barspoon. Use a barspoon to add a hibiscus flower to the bottom of the glass. Top off with additional prosecco. Serve and enjoy.

# cucumber mule

This cocktail is essentially the equivalent of spiked "spa water," which means it's at least almost virtuous. The most obvious nonalcoholic version of this cocktail would be, um, that aforementioned spa water, but you could simply omit the sake or play with nonalcoholic spirits here, too. Either way, the drink's pretty much a guaranteed crowd-pleaser.

**TIME:** 3 MINUTES (PLUS TIME FOR SAKE INFUSION)

**SERVES:** 1

1 English (hothouse) cucumber

3 ounces Cucumber-Infused Sake (recipe follows)

½ ounce fresh lime juice

About 4 ounces ginger beer

Use a vegetable peeler to carefully slice the cucumber lengthwise to make a long, thin ribbon (reserve the remaining cucumber for another use). Wrap the cucumber around the inside the inside of a highball glass. Fill the glass to the top with ice. Add the infused sake, lime juice, and ginger beer; stir well with a barspoon. Serve and enjoy.

## cucumber-infused sake

**MAKES:** 750 ML

2 English (hothouse) cucumbers

1 (750 ml) bottle sake

Trim off and discard the ends of the cucumber. Slice the cucumber in half lengthwise, then roughly slice into pieces. Combine the sliced cucumber and sake in a 1-quart container. Let sit for 24 hours. Strain the infusion into an airtight container. Store the infusion in the refrigerator for 1 week.

# watermelon mojito

This is best described as an upscale mojito that subs prosecco for rum, adds juicy fresh watermelon, and skips spoonfuls of sugar altogether. It's definitely a summer porch drink.

**TIME:** 2 MINUTES
**SERVES:** 1

5 mint sprigs

2½ ounces watermelon juice

½ ounce Ginger Syrup (page 28)

½ ounce fresh lime juice

Prosecco

Fill a highball glass to the top with ice. Clap the mint to release maximum flavor. Add the watermelon juice, ginger syrup, lime juice, and mint to the glass and top off with prosecco. Stir with a barspoon. Serve and enjoy.

# strawberry sunrise

Though its name is somewhat evocative of a sweet elderly couple holding hands as they watch the sunrise, this drink is rather bold in its combination of prosecco, white wine, and tequila. In other words, this beautiful farm-to-table beverage has a bit of a sneaky bite. It's best enjoyed, I'd say, with a lover, though it goes down just as easily with friends over brunch, during an at-home happy hour, or when alone on a Saturday afternoon with your cat/dog/pig/opossum.

**TIME:** 5 MINUTES

**SERVES:** 1

2 strawberries

Ground pink peppercorns

1 ounce tequila

2 ounces sauvignon blanc

1 ounce Strawberry Syrup (page 29)

1½ ounces Strawberry Mint Lemonade (page 230)

1 ounce prosecco

Splash of fresh orange juice

1  Cut the stem out of each strawberry with a "V" cut, then slice each strawberry from top to bottom into ¼-inch-thick slices so that each slice resembles a heart. Take the prettiest slice and cut a small notch in its narrow end. Spread the pink peppercorns on a small plate. Dip one edge of the strawberry slice in the pink pepper until the edge is coated. Set aside, reserving the pink pepper.

2  Fill a wineglass with ice and add the remaining strawberry slices.

3  Add the tequila, sauvignon blanc, strawberry syrup, lemonade, prosecco, and orange juice to the glass. Sprinkle a pinch of pink pepper on top of the drink. Stir with a barspoon. Secure the notched strawberry garnish to the rim of the glass. Serve and enjoy.

# cozy campfire

Mezcal's smokiness partners perfectly in this creamy concoction with cardamom and chocolate bitters, orange juice, and a touch of vanilla. Finally, a winter drink, for all those LA days when it dips below 70 degrees.

**TIME:** 5 MINUTES
**SERVES:** 1

1½ ounces mezcal

1 ounce Cashew Cream (page 18)

½ ounce fresh orange juice

1 ounce Vanilla Syrup (page 28)

8 shakes chocolate bitters

3 shakes cardamom bitters

Wide strip of orange peel, for garnish

Dark chocolate stick, for garnish

1  Fill a small coupe with ice and water to chill the glass. Set aside.

2  Combine the mezcal, cashew cream, orange juice, and vanilla syrup with ice in a cocktail shaker. Shake vigorously. Discard the ice and water from the coupe and strain the cocktail into the chilled glass. Top with the bitters.

3  Fold the orange peel in two and squeeze the essence over the top of the drink. Position the peel and the chocolate stick horizontally atop the coupe. Serve and enjoy.

# tiny piney

This one's named after the restaurant because it's made with fresh rosemary, which gives it a bit of a piney taste . . . in a good way. Cocchi Americano is an Italian apéritif, which means its sweetness offsets the earthiness of the rosemary beautifully. Overall, the mix makes for a potentially too-drinkable drink, so bartender, beware.

**TIME:** 5 MINUTES
**SERVES:** 1

1 sprig rosemary, plus a short sprig for garnish

1½ ounces gin

½ ounce Cocchi Americano

1 ounce fresh lemon juice

¾ ounce Simple Syrup (page 27)

1 ounce soda water

4 shakes cardamom bitters

Strip of lemon peel, for garnish

1  Fill an old-fashioned glass with ice and set aside.

2  Combine the rosemary sprig, gin, Cocchi Americano, lemon juice, and simple syrup with ice in a cocktail shaker. Shake vigorously. Strain into the ice-filled glass. Top with the soda water and add the bitters.

3  Position the rosemary sprig and lemon peel vertically in the glass. Serve and enjoy.

# jitterbug

Few ingredients combine to create as much comfort as do coffee and chocolate. The Jitterbug includes this star duo while also tossing in some coconut, vanilla, and, of course, alcohol, in the form of rum. It's essentially a vacation in a glass, but one so filled with activities that you need a little pick-me-up in order to make it through cocktail hour. Teetotalers can use rum extract mixed with water to simulate the liquor content in this drink.

**TIME:** 5 MINUTES
**SERVES:** 1

2 tablespoons coconut sugar

1½ teaspoons unsweetened cacao powder

1 ounce Vanilla Syrup (page 28)

1½ ounces dark rum

2 ounces coconut cream

3 ounces cold-brew coffee

3 coffee beans, for garnish

1  Mix the coconut sugar and cacao powder on a small round plate until fully combined.

2  Fill a large coupe (10 to 12 ounces) with ice and water to chill the glass, then discard them when the glass is sufficiently cold.

3  Using a sponge or paper towel, moisten the rim of the chilled glass with a bit of vanilla syrup. Turn the glass upside down and dip it into the chocolate coconut sugar, without twisting. Make sure the rim is thoroughly coated.

4  Combine the rum, coconut cream, vanilla syrup, and coffee in a cocktail shaker with ice. Shake vigorously. Strain into the sugared-rim coupe. Garnish with the coffee beans to make a triangle shape. Serve and enjoy.

# matcha do about nothing

A matcha-and-prosecco mix seems to me to be the stuff Instagram dreams are made of (hint, hint #LittlePine #shamelesspromotion #helppussavetheanimals). This drink may not know if it's up or down, but either way, it's packed with antioxidants which, while it may not be the most important consideration of happy hour, I'd imagine is a welcome perk nonetheless. For a virgin version of this drink, simply replace prosecco with sparkling water.

**TIME:** 3 MINUTES

**SERVES:** 1

1 tablespoon sugar

½ teaspoon matcha powder

¼ teaspoon matcha powder

½ ounce hot water

1½ ounces Simple Syrup (page 27)

1½ ounces fresh lemon juice

Prosecco (roughly 2 ounces)

Lemon wheel, for garnish

1  Mix the sugar and ¼ teaspoon of the matcha powder in a small bowl with a dry barspoon until you've made a pale green sugar. Pour the matcha sugar onto a small plate and set aside.

2  Combine the remaining ¼ teaspoon matcha powder and hot water directly in a highball glass. Use an electric frother to whisk the matcha until a smooth, creamy texture is achieved. Add ice to the matcha mixture, filling the glass to the rim. Add the simple syrup and lemon juice. Top off the glass with prosecco. Stir the cocktail with a barspoon, briefly and lightly.

3  Cut a small notch in the lemon wheel. Following the line of the notch, coat half the wheel in matcha sugar by carefully and evenly pressing that half into the matcha sugar. Position the coated lemon wheel on the edge of the glass. Serve and enjoy.

## ACKNOWLEDGMENTS

I'm almost hesitant to write an acknowledgments page, as I'm 99 percent sure I'll accidentally forget to include a bunch of the people who've worked tirelessly to make Little Pine a success. So, if you're one of the people who've worked tirelessly to make Little Pine a success, thank you! Really!

More specifically, I need to thank Leslie Charles, Little Pine's general manager and reigning matriarch. Leslie has been at Little Pine since day one, and without her, we simply wouldn't have a restaurant. To be honest, I've even thought of renaming the restaurant "Leslie's."

We've had dozens of amazing people work in the kitchen, but I would be remiss in not specifically thanking our executive chef, Laura Louise Oates, who gives each day at Little Pine her all and then some. Also, thank you to Amy Noonan, our pastry chef, and Cindy Sukrattawong, our kitchen supervisor, both of whom work long hours and still manage to be creative vegan geniuses. We have also had dozens of remarkable people working front-of-house, but again, I would be remiss in not thanking Honor Nezzo and Jasmine Flores specifically.

With respect to this cookbook, I need to extend my gratitude to Laura Louise Oates, Amy Noonan, and Jason Wood for all their hard work in adapting Little Pine's recipes for the home cook. I also need to thank Erin Nicole Bunch, who has overseen every aspect of producing this cookbook, from the writing to the tasting to the testing to the photography. In many ways, it's more her book than mine, but she's shy and wouldn't want her name in bold on the cover.

And I mean this with profound gratitude and sincerity: thank *you*. Without you, we would have only a cool-looking art deco building and chefs making food for one another. Many of you have supported us since we opened, and in that time, we've served hundreds of thousands of vegan meals, and contributed all our profits to animal rights organizations. By combining Little Pine's profits with my own charitable contributions, we've been able to donate over $500,000 since we first opened.

So, thank you!

index

berry granola bowls, page 69

bagels, *page 51*

*shepardess pie, page 187*